Implementing
Policy Reforms
in LDCs

Implementing Policy Reforms in LDCs

A Strategy for Designing and Effecting Change

Louise G. White

Lynne Rienner Publishers • Boulder & London

Published in the United States of America in 1990 by
Lynne Rienner Publishers, Inc.
1800 30th Street, Boulder, Colorado 80301

and in the United Kingdom by
Lynne Rienner Publishers, Inc.
3 Henrietta Street, Covent Garden, London WC2E 8LU

Library of Congress Cataloging-in-Publication Data
White, Louise G.
    Implementing policy reforms in LDCs : a strategy for designing and
effecting change / by Louise G. White.
        p.   cm.
    Includes bibliographical references and index.
    ISBN 1-155587-214-X (hc : alk. paper)
    ISBN 1-155587-215-8 (pb : alk. paper)
    1. Developing countries—Economic policy I. Title.
HC59.7.W485 1990
338.9'009172'4—dc20   90-8723
                                                         CIP

British Cataloguing in Publication Data
A Cataloguing in Publication record for this book
is available from the British Library.

Printed and bound in the United States of America

The paper used in this publication meets the requirements
of the American National Standard for Permanence of
Paper for Printed Library Materials Z39.48-1984.

To Edward A. White

who models so superbly
the approach described in these pages

Contents

Preface

The political dramas of 1989 were a reminder that it is possible to bring about significant change in a society, even against overwhelming odds. The decade of the 1990s is likely to be a more sobering time as new regimes attempt to institutionalize the political upheavals and take steps to ensure economic growth, freedom, and participation. This book addresses those involved in these changes—leaders and communities within countries and external parties offering assistance. It presents the case for a collaborative and flexible approach to designing and enacting economic change, rather than a top-down social engineering approach.

It is tempting to respond to current economic crises and to the increasing complexity and interdependence in the world by looking for ways to exert control, to rationalize and manage the complexity, and to standardize responses. The opposite response is more persuasive, however. Hierarchical and intellectual systems of management and control cannot keep pace with change. Instead of encouraging standardization, institutions that allow for flexible responses will better enable communities to cope with complexity. Assistance and expertise offered by external parties have to be evaluated against this criterion of flexibility. They can provide much-needed resources —financial, organizational, and intellectual—but they can also be harmful if they are not part of a broad and collaborative process of social and institutional learning.

This study draws on a particular set of experiences to make this case. It looks at efforts by developing nations (LDCs) to cope with severe economic crises, both through their own efforts and through assistance and advice from outsiders. This lesson is clear—orthodox policy reforms to liberalize the economy are necessary but not sufficient to stimulate development. No single economic orthodoxy is applicable to all settings. "Getting the prices right" will stimulate development only if reforms are designed for particular social and political settings, if they are accompanied by steps to make institutions—both public and private—more effective and responsive, and if they take political realities into account.

This kind of change will occur only if local officials collaborate among themselves and with representatives of international institutions to diagnose their problems and design appropriate strategies. The purpose is not to coopt the participants, but to ensure that the reforms address their situations. A collaborative process makes sense politically and intellectually. It places responsibility on those who have the greatest stake in the changes. It elicits firsthand interpretations and critical information about local problems and capacities and allows participants to consider a number of policy responses. It also provides an opportunity for officials to make clear to outsiders that there are limits to their capacity to bring about internal change without additional resources.

A collaborative process makes two important assumptions that differ from commonly held views of policymaking. First, it assumes that individuals are willing to take part in collaborative processes and that they can reason together about their problems and learn from their experiences. This differs from the usual assumption that individuals only pursue their calculated self-interests and that politics consists of competition among interests rather than reasoned discussion. The theory presented here assumes that individuals behave in a variety of ways, and that goal-oriented behavior and self-interest explain only some of their behavior. Individuals may pursue their interests or self-chosen goals, but just as often they try to do what is appropriate in their situation. Second, the theory assumes that political institutions influence behavior. Because people often try to do what is fitting or expected of them, procedures can be designed to encourage rational reflection, dialogue, and learning.[1]

This study draws on these assumptions about individual behavior and the influence of institutions to develop a model of policy inquiry. Thinking strategically to diagnose problems and establish priorities is one important element in this process. Designing a way to cope with problems rather than simply understand them is a second element. Providing a structure to enhance dialogue and substantive learning is a third aspect of the process. Part One of this book establishes the rationale for such a process and elaborates its assumptions. Part Two describes the process, drawing on current field experiences.

The record of carrying out positive social and institutional changes is not reassuring. Failures are particularly evident to those who are sensitive to the weight of culture and history. The problems are compounded when those proposing the changes are outsiders who enjoy a vastly disproportionate amount of the world's assets. A collaborative process can be a weak reed in the face of these realities. Nevertheless, recent events suggest that there are times when it is possible to introduce significant change in a society. The proposed process is designed to capitalize on these opportunities.

---

[1]March and Olsen, 1989, *Rediscovering Institutions*.

Acknowledgments

This study is based on earlier work on implementing policy reforms. In particular, I am grateful to the Bureau of Science and Technology at the United States Agency for International Development (USAID) for research support. Jeanne North and Kenneth Kornher have been especially helpful and insightful in their comments and encouragement; their continuing concern for implementation and management issues over the years has had a major impact on the work of USAID. The responsibility for these words, however, is clearly my own, and does not represent Agency policy.

Larry Graham, formerly with the National Association of Schools of Public Affairs and Administration (NASPAA), also stimulated and encouraged me during a semester I spent with that association. Coralie Bryant provided me with materials, and through many conversations helped me to conceptualize the issue. Elizabeth Shields and Haven North, who are actively and creatively engaged in applying many of the practices described in these pages, were very helpful and encouraging in reflecting on their own experience. Finally, I am grateful to George Mason University for providing me with a semester's faculty leave.

Implementing
Policy Reforms
in LDCs

PART ONE

A PROCESS FOR DESIGNING
AND IMPLEMENTING CHANGE

1

The Changing Agenda
of Policy Reforms in LDCs

The century is closing with a rush of efforts by individual countries to cope with deteriorating economies and financial crises. Within severe constraints imposed by the international economy, governments are exploring wide-ranging, often innovative efforts to improve their economies. Their efforts pose important questions. What role can and should a country's governing bodies play in stimulating its economy? Can outsiders—donors, lenders, trading partners—play a useful role, and if so, what forms of assistance are most helpful?

The world's attention is focused on countries from the socialist bloc as they grapple with these questions. In the meantime, developing countries (LDCs) throughout Africa, Latin America, and Asia have learned some important lessons about economic change. Critically burdened with debt and faltering economies, LDC officials are being strongly encouraged by donors and lenders to expand the private sector and reduce the role of the government in their economies. Liberalizing changes are cautiously being put in place. Although one can point to positive results, particularly in Asia, the overall record is disturbing. Jeffrey Sachs, for example, concluded in 1989 that "the economic crisis of Latin America is intensifying rather than diminishing," and studies of African economies find little evidence of sustained improvement.[1] The economic changes spark serious political protests, weaken emerging democratic regimes, and hurt the poorest groups most of all.[2] The resulting "austerity fatigue" within the LDCs complements the widespread "aid fatigue" afflicting the donor community.

As the 1990s begin, it is clear that the policy reform process involves more complex and longer-term actions than originally thought. Policymakers and administrators find their efforts are aborted or diluted by political, bureaucratic, and social realities. Observers are beginning to ask whether it is even possible to purposefully generate economic change.[3] In response, some parties have been experimenting with an approach to policy change that emphasizes collaboration and strategic planning. Drawing on these efforts this study examines the assumptions in this approach, shows why it is relevant to policy reforms, and describes how to carry it out. The version presented here engages country officials in collaborating among themselves and with others to diagnose situations, develop priorities, and design appropriate policies, institutions, and implementation plans. The chapters in Part Two

3

describe such a strategy; they lay out a series of steps and illustrate the kinds of issues that can be considered. Part One presents the rationale for the strategy and links it to developments in policy analysis. Chapter 1 reviews the record of policy reform efforts in LDCs and analyzes why they have proved so hard to implement.

FROM QUICK FIXES TO LONG-HAUL EFFORTS

LDCs and International Financial Institutions

A number of trends in the 1980s exacerbated the indebtedness of LDCs. Worldwide recession, increased interest rates in the United States, declines in commodity prices, and a contraction of international lending after an explosion of borrowing in the 1970s all combined with internally weak economies and overvalued exchange rates to produce large debts.[4] According to the United Nations, sub-Saharan Africa's indebtedness as a percent of GNP climbed from 57 percent in 1984 to 70 percent in 1987.[5] In Latin America the total debt as a percent of GNP in 1986 was 66 percent for Argentina, 41 percent for Brazil, and 84 percent for Mexico.[6] Many LDC nations found they were repaying more in interest rates than they were receiving through exports, loans, and assistance combined. Translating these figures into their human impact, one study computed that "each one of Africa's 410 million people owed foreigners about $195, or about as much as they earned in six months of toil."[7]

Countries with balance of payments problems can ask the International Monetary Fund (IMF) for a loan or line of credit, in return for which they agree to fulfill conditions designed to stabilize their economies. Typically they try to decrease their fiscal deficits by reducing expenditures and increasing exports. Specific changes include devaluations of inflated currencies to international or border levels, reductions of food subsidies, and restraints on wage increases. Whatever their long-term effect on economic development, the changes impose an immediate and painful austerity on the country, characterized by higher food prices, increases in unemployment, and reduced living standards.

In theory, LDCs develop their own reform agendas. It is commonly known, however, that in practice, creditor governments, commercial banks, and international financial institutions play a dominant role. These often take the initiative in carrying out background studies and encouraging LDC officials to adopt them, and then impose the reforms as conditions for receiving loans. While the IMF has always relied on conditionality in assisting countries with balance of payments problems, in LDCs the conditions virtually are becoming what Nelson describes as "semipermanent arrangements." She adds that "indeed the 1980s has seen external intervention in internal economic policies to a degree unprecedented in terms of the measures addressed and the number of countries involved."[8]

The financial institutions provide assistance to cushion the transition period. The World Bank uses structural adjustment loans (SALs)—quick disbursements to meet balance of payments needs—and sectoral adjustment loans (SECALs)—supports to specific sectors. Both types of loans specify that countries have to adopt policies to meet economic targets. Such policy-based lending makes up approximately 25 percent of the Bank's portfolio, with the rest going to project-based loans. In addition to its traditional lines of credit, the IMF has established special arrangements for the poorest countries—a structural adjustment facility (SAF) and an enhanced structural adjustment facility (ESAF). Although the IMF continues to be primarily concerned with a country's balance of payments, there are signs that it has become more sensitive to the special needs of the most indebted countries and the importance of social factors in explaining weak economic performance.

Implementing Economic Policy Reforms

Liberalizing reforms are widely debated. Most of the controversy deals with the substance of the proposed policy changes and their intended and actual impacts.[9] Increasingly another issue is being raised, namely the difficulties of carrying out the reforms and sustaining them. The record is clearly mixed. In 1988 the World Bank sampled fifty loans to fifteen countries to determine whether governments had complied with donor conditions. It concluded that 60 percent of the conditions had been fully implemented and another 20 percent partially so. The most successful reforms dealt with exchange rates, energy policy, agricultural pricing, financial reforms, and public sector expenditure programs. The least successful were industrial policies, tax reforms, and public enterprise reforms.[10] Nicholas, in another Bank study, found that although adjustment loans "have very rarely been abandoned altogether . . . three-quarters of all adjustment loans are experiencing delays in release [of funds] as a result of delays in fulfillment of agreed conditions."[11] Paul reviewed fifty five SECALs approved by the Bank from 1983 to 1987 and concluded that over one-fifth had serious implementation problems.[12] Joan Nelson, a longtime observer of implementation, chronicles an array of problems. "Even where agreed on actions are taken, governments often fail to take the follow-up measures necessary for more than a brief improvement. Thus an IMF study of exchange-rate adjustments in eleven African nations concludes that the effect of the devaluations were vitiated within one to two years."[13]

Problems in implementing the policy reforms were not widely anticipated. In fact, macroeconomic reforms such as liberalizing exchange rates were appealing because they presumably do not depend on continuing actions by government agencies. The reforms were viewed as relatively "quick fixes" that would virtually implement themselves by generating private capital and stimulating recovery.[14] The nature of reforms has changed substantially during the 1980s, however, and the changes have made implementation far more difficult. According to Nelson, there has been a move from "quick fixes" to a realization that changes, to be effective, involve "long-haul" efforts by all parties concerned.[15] The key change is that economic incentives, although necessary, are no longer seen as sufficient to generate growth and development. Four additional sets of activities increasingly accompany economic policy changes: supporting investments, institutional development, human resources, and social mobilization.

Supporting Investments. By the mid 1980s it was clear that macrolevel financial "fixes," such as stabilization and macroeconomic policy changes, were not sufficient to reverse the increasingly serious economic problems in these countries. Debt was becoming deeper and economies were unable to respond to infusions of aid. In fact, there is troubling evidence that some of the macroeconomic changes have even reduced investments.[16] There is more interest in long-term structural adjustments that include supporting investments within sectors such as agriculture and education. The result is a far more complex set of activities than the original so-called "quick fixes." A World Bank study in 1988 refers to these efforts as "hybrid reforms"—a combination of macroeconomic policies, investment strategies, and project activities.[17] The rationale is simple: price increases are unlikely to be effective unless complementary actions ensure that credit is available, that roads and storage facilities are adequate, that research is relevant to farmer needs, and that extension services are available to women producers, to name only a few critical conditions.[18]

World Bank activities in Guinea illustrate the importance of supporting activities. Guinea, one of the smallest and poorest of the African countries, has been one of the more successful in adopting economic policy reforms.[19] Early in 1986, the Conte military regime adopted a rather remarkable series of changes that went far to liberalize the economy and gave Guinea a reputation as one of the more innovative and flexible countries in Africa. These included devaluation of the currency by 93 percent; introduction of an auction system through which the Central Bank buys and sells foreign exchange; and decontrol of most prices. As a result, prices for agricultural commodities increased and stimulated greater farm production. Farmers planted more coffee trees and increased the acreage of rice under cultivation; in coastal areas the land under cultivation increased by 25 percent.[20] These positive responses, however, came about largely because there was an excess capacity in the economy and room to expand. Future economic improvements will depend on supporting investments—roads, marketing arrangements, credit, improved seed—all necessary before individuals can fully respond to the price incentives.

Institutional Development. A second change is the growing realization that policy reforms require changes in institutions. The term "institutions" includes organizations but has a broader meaning. It refers to rules, norms, and expectations that govern the transactions and relations among peoples. "It is the institutional structure that prevents social orders from coming apart in centrifugal chaos. It is the institutional arrangements that define what can be done, what cannot be done; and who can do what to whom."[21] One source for this more inclusive perspective is economic theory. For economists, institutions include voluntary exchange rules such as markets, hierarchical rules to promote order, rules for joint action through organizations, and rules for voluntary collective action.[22] Another version of institutional theory emphasizes institutions as structures of meaning. See, for example, studies of democratic institutions by March and his associates and analyses of local organizations in LDCs by Esman and Uphoff.[23] For both economists and institutional theorists, institutions are significant forces. They order relationships in various ways, and do not rely simply on public sector organizations.

Institution building has begun to be taken seriously within the development community. A review of fifty-five World Bank sectoral-level reforms found three ways in which reform packages include institutional change: restructuring organizations, deregulating activities, and building a capacity for policy analysis. Restructuring includes divesting organizations of responsibilities, reorganizing units, creating new ones, and strengthening organizations. Regulatory changes include the addition of incentives and safeguards to legal codes, revision of investment codes, new agencies to implement these codes, guarantees that existing regulations are carried out fairly, and information to give entrepreneurs confidence in the stability of the system. Improvements in policy analysis include expanding a unit's capacity to analyze, plan, and evaluate; upgrading skills in foreign trade analysis; training staff; and adding new analytic units.[24]

Such activities reform the public sector rather than simply reduce it. For example, a common policy reform directs officials to privatize parastatals. It is not enough to simply decree privatization, however. Public managers typically need to create an environment that motivates individuals to enter the private sector and ensure that they can perform effectively. They need to be certain that credit is available, guarantee a predictable and supportive legal framework, enforce a rational tax system, protect private property, and provide services such as roads and electricity.[25] A 1988 study of U.S. foreign assistance offers a similarly pragmatic analysis. The public sector needs to assist the private sector, stimulate multiple enterprises, supplement private activities in unprofitable and isolated areas, and monitor whether the benefits are going to those who are intended to receive them.[26]

Actions to improve the quality and variety of seed within Guinea illustrate how institutions can be altered. World Bank staff have been working closely with officials in the Ministry of Rural Development (MDR) to increase the in-country capacity for developing improved seed that is suitable to the different ecological zones. The Bank could have simply provided funds for research and training for staff, relying on existing research institutes. Instead, the Bank concluded that new institutional arrangements were needed, ones designed to respond to regional climactic differences, to directly involve the farmers who would be using the seed, and to offer incentives to be innovative and efficient.

To meet these criteria, the Bank is funding a project to analyze and redesign the institutions for producing seed. The project is establishing Seed Conditioning Centers (SCCs) in several zones. The SCCs purchase seed from the research centers, sell it to private growers to multiply the seed, and then repurchase the seed and sell it to farmers. Once under way the SCCs will be sold to the private sector. At this point the research centers will be working with a network of private sector units and individual farmers. The changes mean that responsibility for developing and conditioning the seed will be diffused among these several parties, but responsibility for overseeing the whole process remains with the research centers. At every step the MDR and its research centers are being cast into entirely new roles—from developing the SCCs, to selling them, to cooperating with them, to monitoring them.[27]

Human Resource Development. There is a third reason for stressing the long-haul nature of the reforms and implementation problems. Increasingly, observers are finding that economic growth depends on the education and health of the populace—on human resource development. Studies in technology transfer emphasize that new technologies cannot simply be transplanted. Agricultural innovations, for example, have to be adapted to new contexts to be effective, and such adaptation depends on an educated work force. Reduced expenditures for education and health, therefore, can be shortsighted and undermine the prospects for growth. The fiscal crises in the 1980s, however, reduced available resources and raised serious doubts about the ability of public sector institutions to provide services or serve the poor.[28] In addition, the poor can actually become worse off in the early stages of economic growth.[29]

The 1980 *World Development Report* stressed that improvements in health and education were important both in their own right and in stimulating economic growth. In the 1990 *World Development Report,* the Bank returned to the issue of poverty and argued that policies to reduce poverty are consistent with economic growth.[30] Realistically, governments have to balance the needs of the poor with those of other groups in the economy and consider the administrative feasibility of various poverty programs. To reconcile long-run growth with the needs of the poor, the report recommends a two-pronged strategy—labor-intensive growth and social services. In countries such as Brazil, growth policies increased the incomes of the poor but services are badly underfunded. In other countries, such as Costa Rica, social services are high but there have been few economic opportunities for the poor. Thailand and Indonesia are examples of countries that have pursued both strategies and have achieved growth and an impressive reduction in poverty. Beyond these policies, the Bank urges that governments will still have to provide a safety net for those who continue to be hurt by the reforms. This option is more likely if the poor increase their participation in political decisions.[31]

Social Mobilization. A fourth reason for viewing reforms as a "long-haul" process, and one that is somewhat more controversial, is the need to mobilize communities, particularly the poor, to participate in growth opportunities. Those who make this claim urge that increased prices alone are insufficient without efforts to reach the more isolated, impoverished, and alienated groups in a community. Korten, for example, observes that the economic success of the "Asian tigers" depended on far more than policies to promote exports. "Exports represent only the tip of the economic iceberg. The *institutions* of the economy that support this tip, and how they were developed, are seldom mentioned by the proponents of export-led growth. Yet, the institutional foundation is basic to the economic strength of Asia's miracle economies. It is this foundation that has allowed their people to share broadly in their economic success and that gives their economies the resilience to adapt to changing economic conditions."[32] Local institutions can capture what Uphoff calls the latent "social energy" in a community. His theory that this energy can be tapped when people work through organizations that they can control has been tested in the Gal Oya Irrigation Project in Sri Lanka. Local workers who were trained as organizers moved into communities, encouraged local farmers to set up their own organizations, and enlisted them in designing, overseeing, and maintaining an irrigation system. Instead of responding to community sentiments, the organizations generated new ones and succeeded in mobilizing the community.[33]

South Korea's highly structured new village program for rural development illustrates a state-led and highly centralized approach to mobilization. Saemaul is a highly organized program through which the central government has organized Korea's 35,000 villages to participate in developing the rural economy and generating resources. The government, working through local bureaucrats, identifies village leaders to organize local councils. The councils meet and select community projects that fit with government-stated priorities. During the early 1970s, the government emphasized village improvements—housing renovations and roads. By 1975 the government was stressing investments in income-generating projects—vegetable gardens and livestock. After 1978 they urged communities to develop welfare projects—community halls and nursery services. Projects are partially paid for by state funds, but gradually the community has assumed more of the responsibility. In 1978 villages were providing 78 percent of the resources for Saemaul projects through labor, land, and cash contributions. By the 1980s the program had become increasingly politicized and corrupt. Prior to that it was credited with mobilizing participation by individuals and communities in economic development and improving the quality of life in rural Korea.[34]

Social mobilization can also be carried out through grassroots movements, and many would argue that these are far more effective in the long run.[35] For example, Zimbabwe has been promoting agricultural productivity through producer price increases and distributions of seed, fertilizer, and credit. Local farmer groups encourage farmers to use and share knowledge and offer assistance with marketing. They reach poor farmers not ordinarily reached by the Ministry of Agriculture and create a demand for government services by encouraging the use of technical information. Thirty-one percent of the farmers working as individuals saw an extension worker, but 86 percent of those who were members of farmer groups did so. Also, by 1984, 5,700 rural savings clubs had been organized in rural villages to assist members in purchasing agricultural supplies. These efforts help to explain why members of farmer organizations consistently outproduce individual farmers, particularly in the drier, more marginal areas.[36]

Table 1.1 lists the several components of policy reforms. The last five items, discussed in the preceding pages, have become increasingly important and indicate why the reforms have become more complex and long-term than originally anticipated.

THE DYNAMICS OF IMPLEMENTATION

According to the above review, economic stabilization and development require supporting investments, institutional development, improved human resources, and mobilization of the poor. What are the prospects for implementing these actions? The most frequent answer to this question notes that implementation is difficult because of the weaknesses in LDC regimes and bureaucracies. It is important, however, to begin by recognizing that the

---

Table 1.1 Elements in Successful Policy Reforms

Macro and sectoral policy changes to liberalize economies

Improved capacity to implement reforms

Supporting investments at sectoral level

Institutional development: private sector and local level

Human resource development

Mobilization to participate in economic development

reforms place onerous demands on governments. The rest of this chapter analyzes first the characteristics of the reforms and second the relevant characteristics of governing systems.

Which characteristics of policies and governing systems are important to look at? The answer varies according to one's view of social change.[37] The dominant view assumes that public policies are responses to social and political forces. This perspective includes both Marxists and pluralists, both of whom assume that officials are constrained and propelled by social and economic forces and have little autonomy. It also includes public choice proponents who assume that officials are driven by their self-interest and need for support. All of these downplay the independent role of government and political commitments. A second perspective assumes that political officials have some autonomy and can influence the policy process. Ideas and policies do more than reflect political pressures. "Elite latitude is present, and there is a 'politics of ideas,' with which leadership attentive to broad publics can take action even against economically powerful interests."[38]

Strategies to implement reforms need to draw on both of these perspectives—the political context that constrains governing officials and the independent role they can play.[39] Taken together, the perspectives suggest that three aspects of the reforms affect their implementation: the fit between proposed reforms and the views and priorities of officials; the social and political context; and the institutional intensity of the reforms. Table 1.2 lays out these characteristics as continua. Policy changes that fall towards the left of each dimension are easier to implement; those that fall towards the right involve more uncertainty and conflict.

Table 1.2 Characteristics of Policy Reforms

	Implementation	
	Easier	Harder
Fit with Perspective of Country Officials		
Agreement on nature of problem	high	low
Understanding of the policy	high	low
Seen as imposed by external parties	no	yes
Social/Political Implications		
Political costs	low	high
Political benefits	high	low
Fit with culture and norms	good	poor
Institutional Intensity		
Requires new tasks, roles, procedures	few	many
Technical complexity	low	high
Involves several organizations	no	yes
Adequacy of existing resources	yes	no

Perspective of Country Officials

Is There Agreement on the Nature of the Problem? Although officials presumably support economic development, they do not necessarily agree on the nature of the problem or the value of such policies as export-led growth, foreign investment, market initiatives, or divestiture. Individualism and competitive markets may run counter to traditional norms. Callaghy poses the question succinctly: "How can governments be convinced to change policies and institutions that neo-orthodoxy believes to be economically damaging or irrational, but which these governments consider politically rational and deeply rooted in local political economy and history?"[40]

Do Officials Understand the Assumptions and Requirements of the Policy? Economic development is difficult to model. Many proposed policy changes are based on complex economic arguments that are difficult to fully understand and are even counterintuitive.[41] Auctions to allocate foreign exchange, presumably one of the "quick fixes," are difficult to comprehend and put in place. Officials have to determine how much foreign exchange is needed and make it available, select among bidding systems, absorb excess liquidity that would otherwise drive up prices, decide how to handle imports of luxury items, and take steps to ensure general confidence in the auction system.

Do Officials and the Public Perceive the Reforms Are Being Imposed on Them? The answer depends both on official policies of the lending institutions and on the attitudes of expatriates working with country officials. One study refers to the "Bank's apparent aspiration to become Sub-Saharan Africa's . . . planning ministry and Platonic Guardian."[42] The international community assumes that external parties need to impose the reforms as conditions for receiving loans and assistance, since the reforms are politically difficult and leaders lack the will to promote unpopular changes. Local perspectives on policy reforms are by definition shortsighted, and it is better to rely on technical experts who are objective and disinterested. Such attitudes by donors give rise to considerable resentment and explain why a number of countries have gone to great lengths to dissociate reforms from policies of lending institutions.[43]

Social and Political Context

What Are the Political Costs and Benefits of Policy Changes? It was widely assumed that the benefits of economic growth would be widespread. Long-term losers would be primarily corrupt government officials and black marketeers, whereas short-term losers such as businessmen and labor would gain in the long run.[44] It has since become clearer that winning and losing is far more complex. Grindle and Thomas find that costs are politically difficult when they are both direct and visible. Privatizing a firm imposes direct costs on the managers, whereas the benefit of increased efficiency is less direct and less visible. Reductions in expenditures provide indirect benefits by reducing the deficit but directly hurt the public.[45] The influence of affected groups is also an important factor. Agricultural policy changes benefit small producers but these groups are unlikely to be organized. The same changes hurt urban interests who are far more politically visible. Another problem is that policy changes may only benefit people in the long run, but the costs are immediate or short-run in nature and thus more apparent. Lindenberg reports that people often perceive that policies hurt them, whether or not they do, and that even if they are told that they will benefit in the long run, they may suspect that the long run will never come.[46]

Does the Policy Change Fit with Cultural Norms? Some policy changes challenge long-standing practices in the community. Policies to protect natural resources may try to alter planting and harvesting practices. Policies to promote export crops may interfere with social norms that link certain crops to familial responsibilities. Even more generally, according to Gilpin "the introduction of market forces and the price mechanism into a society tends to overwhelm and even to dissolve traditional social relations and institutions."[47]

Institutional Intensity [48]

Do Changes Require Organizations to Assume New Roles? New activities require new skills and are almost always threatening. Policies to promote the private sector may require implementing units to change from producing goods and services to stimulating and supporting private units. New roles threaten power positions in an organization and require bureaucrats to give up activities that provided extra income on the side.[49] Similarly, reductions in the civil service threaten long-standing sources of political support.[50] In his study of World Bank SECALs, Paul found that it was relatively easy in trade SECALs to develop export information systems or improve accounting procedures, but that it was difficult to restructure the organization. In general, officials overestimated the capacity of organizations and underestimated the complexity of the reforms.[51]

How Technically Complex Is the Reform? This question poses difficult tradeoffs. Implementation is more likely when problems can be simplified and when uncertainty is reduced, but simplification can make it more difficult to fully adapt reforms to local situations.[52] Recipients have to understand how a technology works in order to adapt it to a new setting.[53] Yet, a full understanding can make it harder to simplify the complexity of a policy response and identify a clear policy position that can be implemented.

Does the Policy Require the Implementing Unit to Work With Other Organizations? A policy change may require a ministry to delegate responsibilities vertically to field units and develop procedures to monitor and communicate with them. Or the change may require a ministry to work horizontally with a number of units and involve coordination, communication, and sharing of resources. Managers may need to establish close linkages with communities and local organizations. Such actions can place implementing units in an entirely new position. They have to work along with and coordinate a variety of units and somehow balance the need for a rational approach to policy with the need to stimulate autonomy and self-reliance within communities.

Are Additional Resources Needed? These include money for recurrent costs and maintenance. Managers have to be fairly creative in searching out additional resources, through user fees, in-kind contributions, private sector contributions, or grants. Resources also include intangibles, such as political support and appropriate technology. Policy changes can require large measures of both.

Most policy changes at the sectoral level fall towards the right of the dimensions listed in Table 1.2. There are almost always value disagreements or conflicting interests. Officials perceive that the changes are being externally imposed and have little sense of ownership. Policies involve complex and uncertain technologies. The changes require managers to undertake new and threatening roles. Losers are visible and organized, there are few available resources to cushion the effects, and the changes go against long-established practices in the community. Policy changes require flexibility, adjustments, and experiments with new roles and responsibilities. Whereas organizations need to carry out routine activities effectively and efficiently, policy changes demand innovative management and organizations that go far beyond "business as usual" practices.

CHARACTERISTICS OF INSTITUTIONS

Implementing policy reforms involves a daunting series of tasks in any setting. The literature on implementation within the United States, for example, is replete with studies documenting implementation difficulties. It is even more difficult for organizations in most Third World situations. A study of policy reforms in Ghana, a country that has been relatively successful in its reform efforts, drew the following conclusions. "The pervasive administrative weakness of the Ghanian state has greatly limited the program. It has affected policy formulation and, above all, implementation. Medium- and long-term government planning has been almost nonexistent. Even basic data gathering and analysis capabilities and accounting skills are very rudimentary. The most effective reform policies have been those that do not involve direct administrative action on a continuous basis."[54] Similar problems exist in Zambia. "Sheer administrative weakness can greatly threaten the effective implementation of an adjustment program. One striking example was the inability of the Zambia government over several years to collect bumper harvests of maize that resulted in part from increases of producer prices which were part of the economic reform package."[55] Long-haul sectoral reforms compound the problems by providing more opportunities for bureaucrats to obstruct the reforms.[56]

Table 1.3 presents the characteristics of LDC governing institutions, using categories similar to those in Table 1.2—perspective of country officials, political context, and institutional capacity.

Table 1.3 Characteristics of LDC Governing Institutions

	Implementation	
	Easier	Harder
Position of Country Officials		
Perception that a crisis exists	Yes	No
Linkage between economic and political agendas	Yes	No
Political Context		
Legitimacy of regime	High	Low
Political institutions to mediate conflict	Yes	No
Institutional Capacity		
Governing capacity	Strong	Weak
Bureaucratic routines and procedures	Adequate	Inadequate
Bureaucratic norms encourage flexibility	Yes	No
Staff trained in analytic and managerial skills	Yes	Limited
Institutions linking implementing units	Yes	No

Position of Country Officials

Is There a Perception That the Country Faces an Economic Crisis?
Callaghy refers to the "trough effect" within LDCs, and argues that countries that have experienced severe economic crisis, or the bottom of a trough, are more open to wrenching changes.[57] According to Horowitz, crises provide an opportunity for elites to exert an influence. "A disproportionate number of

policies are adopted at exceptional times—times of crisis, times when there is a strong demand for change, times when unusual events have immobilized obstacles to new policy or drastically changed the composition of the decision making bodies. At such times, organized interests are frequently ineffective. Ideas for policy become important forces, and elites have a good deal of freedom to put their ideas into operation."[58]

Are Officials Able to Link Economic and Political Agendas? Sustained economic development depends on the ability of political leaders to connect economic restructuring with actions to address social and political pressures. Without this linkage, economic developments can hurt some groups more than others and lead to political opposition. "Liberalization without attention to domestic political stability is likely to prevent successful economic adjustment."[59] This connection was lacking in Zambia, for example, where political elites failed to link the reforms to domestic political pressures, and "the reforms threatened key elements of the ruling coalition, especially civil servants and the parastatals, and aroused considerable popular protest."[60] Some conclude there is a need for strong political institutions, a conclusion that runs counter to other pressures to reduce the role of the state.

Political Context

How Legitimate Is the Regime? Many LDC regimes have had chaotic political histories, with frequent periods of violence and hostile takeovers. As a result, officials are preoccupied with security and are unwilling to encourage further participation or to delegate responsibility to new units. In sub-Saharan Africa, strongman regimes have further weakened political institutions, with their emphasis on "personal rule which corrodes bureaucratic and legal rationality and promote the misallocation of scarce public resources. Such political decay discourages investment and productivity, thereby impeding capitalist development."[61] Hyden attributes the problems in governance in Africa to extreme personalism—the "supremacy of sanctioned arbitrariness."[62] The wrenching irony is that personal rule is a response to the lack of integration in these peasant societies, leading Sandbrook to ask with some poignancy, "What will hold these societies together when the rulers have little in the way of patronage to distribute?"[63]

Are There Institutions Available to Mediate Conflict and Hold Officials Accountable? In addition, there are few alternative institutions within most of these societies that can either check or support government agencies. There are typically no effective opposition parties, no legislative accountability, no active press, and a weak middle class and private sector. One result is widespread corruption within bureaucracies and an accompanying alienation and cynicism about bureaucracies among the public at large.[64]

Institutional Capacity

Is There a Capacity to Govern? LDC institutions are notoriously weak. Many were left totally unprepared for self-governance by colonial powers and they inherited hierarchical and centralized institutions. These thrive on routinized bureaucratic procedures and "going by the book" rather than problem solving. For the most part, regimes have retained these rigid hierarchies, replete with stultifying red tape, and have even made them more cumbersome by hiring unneeded civil servants as a form of patronage. At the same time, according to Hyden, the problem is not an excess of bureaucracy, but one that is completely inadequate to the task of governing.[65]

Are Bureaucratic Procedures Adequate? Many reforms depend on fairly routine bureaucratic practices—the ability to collect information, communicate with different units, get supplies to the right place on time, monitor activities, and keep financial records. Such practices are particularly salient with sectoral adjustment reforms that involve a number of agencies and other organizations. Policies to reduce the number of civil servants, for example, depend on having a list of government employees, a capacity for testing personnel, and procedures for supervising and promoting individuals. According to Dichter, these very basic procedures involving accounting, recruitment, and personnel are the place to begin in improving capacity for development.[66]

A well-documented case involving operational problems occurred in Zambia in late 1986. Officials decided to remove price subsidies on breakfast meal maize, the type purchased by the middle class, while retaining subsidies on mealie meal, the type purchased by the poor. The problem was how to manage the subsidy payments. The proposed system required millers to buy all their maize at the full price. The government would give them a subsidy for the maize they ground into mealie meal. The millers knew that the government had no procedures to pass on the subsidies and so they chose to grind all the maize into breakfast meal, for which they knew they could get the higher price. The result was higher prices for the breakfast meal, a severe shortage of mealie meal, and major riots in several areas.[67]

Do Bureaucratic Norms Encourage Flexibility and Programmatic Thinking? Typically the norms within LDC organizations discourage innovation. Officials are not used to thinking of policy as a way to solve problems or of implementation in terms of performance. They do not think programmatically or relate separate projects to broader program goals. They tend not to be risk takers or to consider and compare alternative strategies. They are not accustomed to rewarding performance or to linking salaries and job level with performance.[68]

Are Staff Trained with Relevant Analytic and Managerial Skills and in a Position to Use Them? In general, there is a dearth of well-trained people to work in agencies. Those who are trained find salaries in the public sector far too low and find work elsewhere. If they do work in the public sector, they are not well used and end up supervising large numbers of lower-level civil servants in doing routine tasks.[69] The very low pay scales in most of these countries tempt them to use their jobs to exact private payments, with the result that graft flourishes throughout the system.[70]

Are There Procedures to Link Implementing Units? Interministerial coordination is always difficult, but few LDCs have procedures for linking officials, particularly at the midlevel where many operational decisions are made.

The discussion indicates that most LDC governing institutions fall toward the right of the dimensions in Table 1.3. The result is that implementation is exceedingly difficult. It is hard for officials to link economic and political agendas, there are limited mechanisms for resolving conflicts, and there is a very limited capacity for the routine activities of governance.

CONCLUSIONS

Policy changes associated with structural adjustments are characterized by uncertainty and frequently by norms and expectations that run counter to the policy goals of country officials. They are also fraught with political perils and place enormous demands on government agencies. At the same time, the existing governing organizations are notoriously ill-suited for dealing with these demands—for promoting changes, for remaining flexible, for experimenting, for adopting a problem-solving mode, and for working creatively with groups in their environment.

Given these evident problems, is it reasonable to assume that LDC officials, even with external assistance, can successfully design and adopt the kinds of changes required to carry out policy reforms? Chapter 2 lays the basis for answering this question by examining the lessons of the policy reform efforts to date, and considering to what extent participants are learning from these lessons, and what problems they continue to face in doing so. The remainder of the study proposes a strategy for pursuing change that specifically draws from these lessons. Chapter 3 compares strategies for addressing the lessons and proposes a process approach to change that draws from strategic thinking and management. Chapter 4 turns to the fields of policy analysis and management theory and suggests that a strategic approach to policy reforms should be based on an inquiry approach to analysis. Chapter 5 continues the description of the process by discussing various techniques for putting the process in place.

NOTES

1. Sachs, 1989, *New Approaches*, 5. For studies of Africa see the essays in J. Nelson, 1989, *Fragile Coalitions*.
2. Cornia, et al., 1987, *Adjustment with a Human Face;* Lewis, 1988, *Strengthening the Poor,* 23.
3. Callaghy, 1989, "Toward State Capability."
4. Sachs, 1989, *New Approaches*.
5. *Wall Street Journal,* September 21, 1988.
6. Kaufman, 1989, "Politics."
7. Haykin, 1987, *Policy Reform Programs*, 4.
8. J. Nelson, 1989, "Long-Haul Economic Reform," 18.
9. Recent examples include World Bank, 1988, *Adjustment Lending;* Nicholas, 1988, *World Bank's Lending*. A more critical assessment is found in Cornia et al., 1987, *Adjustment with a Human Face*.
10. World Bank, 1988, *Adjustment Lending,* 89–90; McCleary, 1989, "Policy Implementation," 32.
11. Nicholas, 1988, *World Bank's Lending,* x, 9–14.
12. Paul, 1989, "Institutional Reforms."
13. J. Nelson, 1986, "Diplomacy of Policy Based Lending," 78.
14. Sachs, 1989, *New Approaches;* J. Nelson, 1989, "Long-Haul Economic Reform."
15. J. Nelson, 1989, "Long-Haul Economic Reform."
16. World Bank, 1988, *Adjustment Lending,* 24.
17. World Bank, 1988, *Adjustment Lending,* 11.
18. World Bank, 1988, *Adjustment Lending;* Lele, et al., 1989, *Cotton in Africa,* 6.
19. USAID, 1987, *Interim Country Development,* 12.
20. This is the conclusion of field observations and is reported in USAID, 1987, 12.
21. Daniel Bromley, 1985. Commenting at a workshop at USAID, he traces the concept of institutions back to John Commons's work on institutional economics in 1934.
22. Buchanan and Tullock, 1962, *Calculus;* Nicholson, 1989, "State of the Art," 20; Kiser and Ostrom, 1982, "Three Worlds."
23. March and Olsen, 1989, *Rediscovering Institutions,* 52; Esman and Uphoff, 1984, *Local Organizations,* 21–23.
24. Paul, 1989, "Institutional Reforms," 11–15.
25. This list is taken from Sandbrook, 1986, "State and Economic Stagnation," 320. He bases it on actions taken by public sectors in the newly industralizing countries (NICs).
26. Office of Technology Assessment, 1988, *Enhancing Agriculture,* 139–140.
27. World Bank, 1987, *National Seeds Project*.
28. World Bank, 1989b, *Sub-Saharan Africa,* especially chapter 3.
29. Cornia, et al., 1987, *Adjustment with a Human Face*.
30. World Bank, 1990, *World Development Report,* Overview.
31. World Bank, 1990, *World Development Report*.
32. Korten, 1990, *Getting to the 21st Century*.
33. Uphoff, 1985, "Peoples' Participation"; 1987, "Social Energy." Uphoff and colleagues report evidence based on survey research that farmers are most apt to participate when water supply is relatively scarce rather than absolutely scarce or abundant. Uphoff et al., 1990.
34. Lee, 1981, *New Community*. See especially essays by Jin Hwan Park, Ki

Hyuk Park, and Ronald Aqua. Boyer and Ahn, 1989, "Local Government."

35. For example, see Esman and Uphoff, 1984, *Local Organizations.*

36. Bratton, 1989b, "Government-NGO Relations"; Bratton, 1986, "Farmer Organizations."

37. Skocpol, 1985, "Bringing the State Back In"; Grindle and Thomas, 1989, "Policy Makers," 216–221; White, 1990d, "Global Policy Studies"; March and Olsen, 1984, "The New Institutionalism."

38. D. Horowitz, 1989, "Policy Process," 207. This emphasis on the power of ideas is also found in Esman and Uphoff, 1984, *Local Organization;* and Korten, 1984, "Strategic Organization."

39. Grindle and Thomas, 1989, "Policy Makers."

40. Callaghy, 1989, "Toward State Capability," 116. See also Kahler, 1989, "International Financial Institutions."

41. J. Nelson, 1984, "Political Economy."

42. Green and Allison, 1986, "World Bank's Agenda," 72.

43. For example, Nigeria, as described in Callaghy, 1990, "State and Market"; and Latin American countries as described in Sachs, 1989, *New Approaches.*

44. Lindenberg, 1989, "Economic Adjustment," 365.

45. Grindle and Thomas, 1989, "Policy Makers."

46. Lindenberg, 1989, "Economic Adjustment."

47. Gilpin, 1987, *Political Economy,* 22; Gellar, 1985, "Pitfalls."

48. This variable appears throughout the literature. For example, see Paul, 1989, "Institutional Reforms."

49. Nicholson and Connerley, 1989, describe the imperatives of rent seeking, "Impending Crisis," 385–425.

50. J. Nelson, 1989, "Long-Haul Economic Reform," 11.

51. Paul, 1989, "Institutional Reforms," 36.

52. Brewer and deLeon, 1983, *Foundations of Policy Analysis,* 96–99.

53. R. Nelson, 1989, "On Technological Capabilities." He goes on to challenge the very concept of "technology transfer" because it suggests that recipients are passive and does not stress understanding enough.

54. Callaghy, 1990, "State and Market." See also Grindle, 1980 for an overview of implementation problems.

55. Callaghy, 1990, "State and Market."

56. J. Nelson, 1989, "Long-Haul Economic Reforms."

57. Callaghy, 1990, "State and Market"; Grindle and Thomas, 1989, "Policy Makers," stress the importance of perceptions of crisis.

58. D. Horowitz, 1989, "Policy Process," 205. Grindle and Thomas also emphasize the importance of "crisis" versus "politics-as-usual," 1989, "Policy Makers," 229.

59. Callaghy, 1989, "Toward State Capability," 119. He calls this linkatge "embedded liberalism," and connects it to Gilpin's concept of "benign mercantilism," Gilpin, 1987, *Political Economy,* 404–405.

60. Callaghy, 1989, "Toward State Capability," 126.

61. Sandbrook, 1986, "State and Economic Stagnation," 321.

62. Hyden, 19833, *No Shortcuts,* 77.

63. Sandbrook, "State and Economic Stagnation," 330.

64. Hyden, 19833, *No Shortcuts,* notes that in many African countries the government is an irrelevance to large numbers of the populace.

65. Hyden, 1983, *No Shortcuts.*

66. Dichter, 1987, *Development Management.*

67. Kydd, 1986, "Changes in Zambian Agricultural Policy"; Weidemann, 1987,

Zambian Agriculture; Sukin, 1987, "Zambia."

68. These characteristics are documented in many cases. See, for example, the analysis of government organizations in Guinea reported by Diallo et al., 1988, "Organization Development"; Brinkerhoff and Goldsmith, 1988, "Challenge of Administrative Reform"; and the cases cited by Klitgaard, 1989, "Incentive Myopia," 447–459.

69. Meesook and Suebsaeng, 1985, "Wage Policy."

70. Nicholson and Connerly, 1989.

2

Lessons for
Implementing Policy Changes

Experiences with policy reforms over the past decade offer a number of lessons about designing, implementing, and assisting economic changes. Some were learned from painful failures, others from more successful efforts. This chapter reviews these, looking both at lessons for country officials and for external parties offering assistance.

Economic Policy Reforms Offer
Necessary But Insufficient Incentives to Change

Externally assisted reform has a long history in LDCs. Early efforts used transfers of resources, new technology, or training to promote development. Later there was more attention to political and bureaucratic reforms.[1] Recent reformers are correct that policy incentives are critical ingredients in the development process, that "getting the prices right" is essential. Farmers are unlikely to use a new technology if policy keeps commodity prices low. Similarly, entrepreneurs are unlikely to undertake risks if central government rules discourage investments. Policy incentives are particularly effective in stimulating people to protect natural resources. According to property theory, for example, individuals will conserve property when it is removed from the public realm and they can benefit directly from their conservation efforts.[2]

Individuals also respond to social and political incentives, however, and an economic emphasis on price incentives is incomplete. A study of agricultural policy changes in Senegal in 1984 found that higher prices do not necessarily lead to more production. Peasants were more concerned with reducing risks than in increasing their cash income and therefore planted a variety of crops irrespective of market prices. Cultural practices also had an influence. Senegalese peasants do not view millet solely as a cash crop. They grow it partly for its subsistence value and also to fulfill communal and religious commitments. In this case, price increases to stimulate production do not have as great an effect as economists assume.[3]

The debate about the sufficiency of macro policy changes is illustrated by efforts to explain why the East Asian newly industrializing countries (NICs) have been so successful in pursuing economic growth. Early estimates attributed growth rates to market incentives and the emphasis on exports. Recent research, however, notes the strong national commitment to economic growth in these countries and the equally strong presence of the state in brokering access to capital and technology and in implementing the reforms.[4] Other research suggests that land reform and local institutions help to explain the economic success of the NICs. Korten points to the extensive development of local institutions in these countries, to their land reform policies that gave people throughout the society a stake in economic change, and to the strong role of the government in promoting education.[5]

Reforms Have to Reflect Particular Social, Economic, and Political Contexts

Despite evidence that price incentives and market arrangements enhance development, there is no single package of reforms that can be applied across the board. Mosley's study of Kenyan agriculture demonstrates that production problems in that country did not stem from overvalued currencies, from pricing policies, or from taxes on exports, despite the predictions of orthodox economics. A close study of events shows particular problems unique to Kenya, many of which can be traced to past donor practices.[6] The above discussion of farming in Senegal indicates the importance of cultural and social practices. Earlier discussions about the political rationality of reforms suggest that particular political circumstances need to be considered. Based on a review of twelve cases where reforms were attempted, Grindle and Thomas add that particular circumstances offer different kinds of opportunities, and officials should take advantage of these.[7] Donors are getting the message. The World Bank, for example, increasingly relies on in-depth, country-specific, studies, known as "country economic and sector work" (CESW).[8]

Attention to social and political issues, however, remains very uneven.[9] In his review of institutional analysis carried out by the World Bank, Paul emphasized that donors continue to have a technical bias. "In general, institutional diagnosis [in Bank studies] focused on the technical aspects of service delivery and of institutions. . . . The impact of interest groups on the workings of the institutions, the likely resistance to reforms from the political or bureaucratic fronts and an assessment of the risks involved in the proposed reforms seem to have been neglected."[10] Lancaster observes that although many donor officials recognize the importance of different contexts, they still assume that "the same kinds of reforms will have roughly similar impacts in different societies; and that policy reforms can, with enough time, work to promote recovery and growth." She counters that political economists, less universalistic and less optimistic, have an important perspective to offer. "They view government structures and policies as reflective of historical, social, and political phenomena, including conflicts among ethnic, regional, or economic groups and classes for power."[11]

Interest in political contexts has been heightened by the growth of new democracies and their vulnerability to popular discontents. Government officials have to balance domestic groups while mediating between internal groups and international bodies. Because these are difficult tasks, reformers need to temper their expectations and not expect too many changes at once. Heightened expectations in new democratic regimes give new leaders little room in which to maneuver.[12] Those who want to pursue both democracy and economic development have to first develop trust in the state through policies that contain prices and promote participatory institutions.[13] Lindenberg uses four measures of political success: remaining in office, handling social conflict, passing stabilization measures, and protecting the most vulnerable groups. Costa Rica, South Korea, and Zimbabwe are among the few that have met all four of these criteria.[14]

There Is No Single Economic Orthodox Solution; Different Perspectives Can Be Valid

Both of the above lessons challenge the belief that a single economic orthodoxy applies to all situations. A review of reforms in eighteen countries documents that economists hold different views about development. Economists, for example, differ about the causes of inflation and the respective influence of monetary and structural forces. The IMF and World Bank, however, tend to overlook such differences. They generally discount structural factors and assume that monetary policy explains inflation.[15] The Economic Commission for Africa (ECA) counters that factors such as weather, commodity prices, and the debt situation also need to be taken into account in explaining economic patterns.[16]

The lesson is that alternative views may reflect honest disagreements about local issues and are not necessarily defensive postures governed by political self-interest. Paul Streeten, for example, warns that "economics is not a science" and that donors and local officials can reasonably disagree on a number of points. It is reasonable to differ about the likely effects of devaluation or of increases in oil prices. Streeten continues that there are a number of reasons for the differences. Political officials ascribe to a variety of values at the same time, whereas donor officials are more narrowly attuned to the value of efficiency. The two groups also have different time horizons, which in turn produce different views about affordable risks.[17]

Joan Nelson describes the range of the debate. "Many economists have doubts about how fast and far export promotion and import liberalization should be pushed in particular countries, nor can small countries' concerns about food security or broader vulnerability to international shocks be lightly dismissed. And despite the new global consensus that extensive central planning works badly, there is room for wide variation in views and practice regarding the appropriate role of the state in the economy." The differences are even more apparent with sectoral adjustments and investment strategies. Usually there is widespread consensus that stabilization and macroreforms are desirable. "But when the agenda broadens to include structural changes and medium-term development strategies, different views regarding goals, values, and priorities become salient and technical consensus wanes."[18]

Those Implementing the Reforms Need to Have Some Discretion for Adjusting and Sequencing the Changes

Since local circumstances influence how reforms will be played out, successful implementation of the reforms requires taking these differences into account. Those in charge of implementing the reforms need to have some discretion for adapting them, since implementation problems may indicate poorly formulated policies. An external review of activities by the United States Agency for International Development (USAID) commends the Agency for promoting flexibility. "Lessons learned from planning and implementing past projects and programs have led to calls for less pre-planning and more flexibility to change activities during project implementation. Critics argue that excessive pre-planning leads to problems because plans may be over four years old before being initiated or there may be a reluctance to change pre-planned activities despite significant changed circumstances. 'Rolling designs' have been proposed as an alternative. In these, an activity, though still planned in advance, can be changed by its implementors to respond to local capabilities and constraints."[19]

This lesson has caveats attached. Community elites can hijack policies, and bureaucrats and political officials can reorient them to suit their immediate purposes. The hybrid reforms and sectoral programs described in Chapter 1 provide multiple opportunities for groups to coopt or divert policy changes. "Rent seeking" is a constant temptation. When a good is supplied below its real market value, rents can easily be charged by those who control the supply, whether public agencies, businesspeople or farmers. "Rents can also be derived where government regulatory policies limit business activities: e.g., rights to cut timber, permits to manufacture certain products, entry to the civil service. [Such limits] produce an artificial shortage, or even monopoly, of the good or service and substantial profits to those who can secure a license."[20]

Strong State Support Is Needed to Make the Reforms Work; The Point Is to Change the Role of the State, Not Necessarily to Reduce It

Many of the reform proposals try to reduce the role of the state and rely more on the market. States, however, have played a major role in promoting economic development. Karl Polanyi and Douglass North are among those who show that the rise of capitalism in the West benefitted from strong state actions.[21] Recent studies confirm that many of the most striking cases of economic reform have taken place in countries with strong states. Chu finds that South Korea's "economic miracle" was partially a product of a strong state presence. The bureaucracy had a coherent ideology, there were policy networks linking the bureaucracy with the private sector, and social groups expected the government to stimulate a strong economy.[22] Callaghy stresses links with social and economic forces and notes that the "success or failure of adjustment efforts depends on a government's ability to insulate itself—and buffer against and adjust to—threatening political, societal, and international pressures." Chile and Mexico are countries that were able to do this, but most sub-Saharan countries in Africa have not managed this balancing act.[23]

The growing interest in the role of the state has sparked a search for different models of state activity. The Nordic social market model includes a strong and unencumbered private sector with state responsibility for developing human resources and providing safety nets.[24] A second model is represented by small European democracies such as Austria that pursue a liberal foreign trade but rely on the government to subsidize domestic investment and maintain full employment.[25] These countries all have strong democratic political institutions that are able to hold the state accountable. Since these are lacking in many LDCs, the above models have to be adopted judiciously.

Reformers Need to Develop Alternative Institutions and Look for Opportunities to Devolve Responsibility for Programs to Other Units

This lesson is an important corollary to the need for a strong supportive state and the value of discretion during implementation. There is a value in developing and supporting institutions throughout the society, particularly in the private and voluntary sectors. Korten, Uphoff, and Esman are among those who have written extensively about the need to mobilize community groups and work through local organizations to reach the poor and to counter the rigidities of public bureaucracies.[26] Public choice theorists draw similar lessons. Diffusing authority and stimulating competition are ways to avoid the debilitating red tape and rent seeking associated with bureaucracies.[27]

These points were originally made in the context of project assistance, but they are equally applicable to the current emphasis on program funding and hybrid reforms.

Donors are caught in an interesting paradox—they try to both limit the role of the state in the economy and strengthen the capacity of the central planning units of the state to implement reforms. This lesson emphasizes the need for a variety of public and private institutions with the capacity to carry out policy reforms. It warns that in situations where political institutions are weak, centralized authority can be cumbersome and stifling.

Political Leadership Can Promote Change

Traditional studies of LDCs emphasize the overwhelming constraints, both internal and external, on independent political action. Yet there is evidence that leaders can bring about change. Cases indicate that policy elites are not merely brokers of different interests. Nor are they necessarily obstructionists or passive players in the reform process. Government officials do take actions that bring about changes to promote economic development in their societies. Elites are able to shape the process to some extent, even as they have to work within the constraints of the social and economic setting. One review of cases concluded that leaders "often articulated goals for their societies and for the activities of the state. Goals frequently reflected the predispositions of decision makers which were in turn often influenced by bureaucratic positions, professional training, and experiential learning. The cases also indicate that policy elites represented the concerns of a particular regime and shared a sense of the importance of regime survival and their own responsibility for it."[28]

The countries in which leaders have been most successful in promoting reforms experienced a devastating economic crisis. Crises change the political calculus of officials. According to Grindle and Thomas, in crisis situations, regime survival and international pressures play a larger role than they do in noncrisis situations.[29] Ghana, Costa Rica, Sri Lanka, and Guinea illustrate countries where severe crises have set the stage for broad acceptance of major changes. It is important, however, that leaders move decisively to take advantage of what is usually a rather brief grace period.[30] Officials do not necessarily perceive a crisis even if there is one. Callaghy observes that officials in sub-Saharan Africa, in particular, do not generally appreciate how marginal they have become in the international economy, and this failure prevents them from facing their economic problems.[31]

Conditionality Has Not Been
Effective and Generates Resentment

Conditionality does not have a very positive record in promoting reforms, and it involves very intrusive monitoring that can become a major irritant.[32]

Conditionality works best for specific actions that can be carried out fairly easily and quickly; it works less well for longer-range sectoral adjustments. The problems can arise during implementation. Political leaders may agree to conditions in order to receive needed funds, but administrators whose support is necessary to implement them probably have fewer incentives to adhere to them.[33] Interestingly, conditionality encourages donors to inflate their analyses of the prospects for recovery. The IMF pretends that the funds can be repaid within its time limits while the Bank tends to be optimistic "to encourage the government and perhaps to promote more financing from bilateral and commercial sources." Such overoptimism leads to shortfalls which further discredit officials and erode public confidence.[34]

Further, conditionality causes resentment. Even if they perceive a crisis situation, and even if they agree on the general outline of needed reforms, country officials often resent the role of external bodies. Callaghy's description of Ghana, a country that has been relatively successful in implementing reforms, makes the point. "The Fund, Bank, and donor countries believe that expatriate personnel and their skills are necessary to ensure that their funds are used wisely. The World Bank, for example, sent more than 40 missions to Ghana in 1987. Without much of this expatriate work, the adjustment effort would not have progressed nearly so far, but a real political problem has been created in the process. The often intense resentment of the role of expatriates has clearly identified the program with external actors and weakened its legitimacy among key groups in Ghana."[35]

This fear of intrusiveness has increased as donors have moved from project-based assistance to program lending, a move that forces them to become more involved in internal policy choices. Efforts to improve the capacity of the ministries of finance and planning in Zambia, for example, were deeply resisted because officials did not want expatriates to interfere in these central policymaking bodies.[36]

Dialogues as Two-Way Exchange Can Improve the Prospects of the Reforms

Participation in a dialogue encourages greater commitment by local officials. There are other reasons for dialogues also. Local officials are an important source of contextual information and need to have a major role in shaping the choice of economic policies and the sequencing of the changes. Dialogues provide an opportunity to consider alternative perspectives on economic change. Donors are apt to view dialogues as occasions for educating local officials about neo-orthodox approaches. Given the lessons in this chapter, they are better seen as opportunities to explore options.[37] The earlier lesson that there are a number of valid models of economic development assumes that dialogues provide an opportunity for mutual exchange about key problems as well as for educating participants about solutions.

Donors have adjusted their procedures to encourage more genuine dialogue.[38] A World Bank study urges that "government officials should be fully involved, and Bank officials should, where appropriate, support the process of consensus building through seminars or other means." The Bank relies increasingly on Policy Framework Papers (PFPs) "developed by governments in close collaboration with the Bank and the Fund."[39] Even when formal statements are didactic, actual conversations are more open and "Bank personnel show far more uncertainty and realization that actual decisions are complex, imperfect choices with no unique right answers."[40] Sectoral reforms also offer an opportunity to negotiate about packages of reforms and sequencing, items that are harder to raise in a "quick-fix" scenario.

There are a number of proposals for improving the dialogue process. Lindenberg suggests several: begin with the easier issues, and those where there is more consensus; bring together donor officials with opposing interests; look for areas where donors can be flexible; educate country officials about donor decision processes.[41] Nelson wants to include more parties, develop new channels, and ensure that the conversations are two-way.[42] Kahler recommends including those both above and below the key operating ministers who are usually involved. He also proposes joint research on key issues by Bank staff and local government agencies, the use of neutral outside experts, and stronger donor missions in-country.[43]

Donors Are Often Part of the Problem

Several donor characteristics impede genuine dialogues. International financial institutions are under severe pressures to move money, and the result is "urgent, high-stakes negotiations." Instead of encouraging genuine dialogues, the pressures "create strong incentives for what Callaghy calls 'ritual dances'—in which hard-pressed governments tell international institutions what they have been instructed to say, and the institutions in turn pretend to believe what they hear."[44] In addition, the IMF and Bank spend a lot of time trying to arrive at a consensus between themselves, giving them less room to negotiate with country officials.

An analysis of reforms in Kenya notes that donors emphasize management weaknesses within the country to explain reform failures, especially the inability of public agencies to spend their funds. A closer analysis suggests that such financial problems span four analytically separate issues, not all of which are internal. (1) Kenyan accounting procedures are inefficient and can cause delays. (2) The government does not have funds in its recurrent budget to handle a problem. (3) Donor conditions impose delays. Increasingly, "timely disbursement of money is prevented by disagreements between donor and recipient over matters of more general economic policy."[45]

(4) Macroeconomic conditions lead to severe budgetary shortfalls.

Internal procedures and external demands for accountability also make it hard for donors to allow flexible and open-ended reform plans. They are under considerable pressures to produce immediate and clear results. As a recent study of assistance observed, "All organizations tend to avoid such complexity; those in the public eye, with little external support, have all the more reason to emphasize activities where they have some reasonable and predictable chances of success."[46] These pressures explain the preference for narrow, technocratic activities, rather than more complex institutional changes. Donors find it easier to work with technocrats from host countries and encourage such people to assume responsible positions at the expense of those who have come up through political channels.[47]

An experience in Haiti illustrates the problem when well-intentioned rules interfere with institutional change. An expatriate contractor for a donor-funded education program worked closely with a group of educators in Haiti to design a plan to improve private education in that country. The group not only contributed to the design but mobilized considerable political support for the project. Donor regulations, however, specified that there would have to be an open, competitive bidding for a contract to implement the plan. USAID officials within Haiti noted, however, that such a process would undermine the group that had invested so much and would "seriously threaten our working relationships in this politically charged environment." A compromise was reached, but the incident illustrates how easily procedural requirements can impede local responsibility for development.

Table 2.1 Lessons from Experiences with Policy Reforms

Economic policy reforms offer necessary but insufficient incentives to change.

Reforms have to reflect particular social, economic, and political contexts.

There is no single economic orthodox solution; different perspectives can be valid.

Those implementing the reforms need to have some discretion for adjusting and sequencing the changes.

Strong state support is needed to make the reforms work; the point is to change the role of the state, not necessarily to reduce it.

Reformers need to develop alternative institutions and look for opportunities to devolve responsibility for programs to other units.

Political leadership can promote change.

Conditionality has not been effective and generates resentment.

Dialogues as two–way exchange can improve the prospects of the reforms.

Donors are often part of the problem.

Conclusions

The process of inducing economic development involves both macrolevel economic policy changes as well as broad institutional changes throughout a society. How does one go about promoting these kinds of change, particularly in weak and fractious regimes? It is not possible to identify ahead of time the exact problems or the best strategy for all settings. Rather, these need to grow out of an analysis of the local situation and the demands of the particular policy task. The social, economic, and political context is critical. Those in charge need to take this setting seriously, anticipate the problems it poses, and look for possible opportunities. Policy changes are more apt to be appropriate to the situation and have a better chance of being implemented if local officials are part of the planning process and if alternative perspectives are taken seriously from the outset.

The following chapter examines strategies for introducing change and proposes a process for designing and implementing policy reforms. Although LDC officials and international financial institutions are beginning to address the problems posed in Chapter 1, the results are uneven. The proposed strategy suggests a way to address the lessons in this chapter more systematically.

NOTES

1. Rondinelli, 1987, *Development Administration,* discusses recent efforts; Bryant and White, 1982, *Managing Development,* review changes since the 1950s.
2. Thomson, 1981, "Public Choice Analysis"; Timberlake, 1985, *Africa in Crisis.*
3. Gellar, 1985, "Pitfalls."
4. Deyo, 1987, "Coalitions"; Johnson, 1987, "Political Institutions"; Bradford, 1986, "East Asian 'Models.'"
5. Korten, 1990 *Getting to the 21st Century,* cites Uphoff's edited collection of studies of institutionalization in South Asia, 1982.
6. Mosely, 1986, "Agricultural Performance."
7. Grindle and Thomas, 1989, "Policy Makers."
8. Nicholas, 1988, *World Bank's Lending,* 4. See also Helleiner, 1986b, "Policy-Based Program Lending."
9. Vondal, 1987, "A Review."
10. Paul, 1989, "Institutional Reforms," 23.
11. Lancaster, 1988, "Political Economy," 173.
12. Haggard and Kaufman, 1989, "Politics"; J. Nelson, 1989, "Long-Haul Economic Reform," 16.
13. Whitehead, 1989, "Democratization."
14. Lindenberg, 1989, "Economic Adjustment," 378.
15. Taylor, 1987, "IMF Conditionality."
16. ECA, 1989, *African Alternative,* 3–9; Mosely, 1986, "Agricultural Performance."
17. Streeten, 1987, "Structural Adjustment," 1480f. Helleiner, 1986b, "Policy-Based Program Lending," 62, argues that Bank research is designed to confirm its

biases and fails to explore alternative arguments.

18. J. Nelson, 1989, "Long-Haul Economic Reform," 15. See also Helleiner, 1986b, "Program Lending."

19. Office of Technology Assessment, 1988, *Enhancing Agriculture,* 152, fn. 4. See also Brinkerhoff and Ingle, 1989, "Structured Flexibility."

20. Nicholson and Connerley, 1989, "Crisis," 399–400.

21. Polanyi, 1944, *Transformation;* North, 1981, *Structure and Change.*

22. Chu, 1989, "State Structure."

23. Callaghy, 1989, "State Capability," 120.

24. Mitra, 1989, "Social Market Economy."

25. Katzenstein, 1985, "Small Nations."

26. Korten, 1990, *Getting to the 21st Century;* Uphoff, 1986, *Local Institutional Development;* Esman and Uphoff, 1984, *Local Organizations.*

27. Nicholson and Connerley, 1989, "Impending Crisis"; Associates in Rural Development, 1989, *Bangladesh.*

28. Grindle and Thomas, 1989, "Policy Makers," 222.

29. Grindle and Thomas, 1989, "Policy Makers."

30. Lindenberg, 1989, "Making Economic Adjustment Work," 377, 379. He cites Cornia et al., 1987, *Adjustment with a Human Face,* and Callaghy, 1990, "State and Market."

31. Callaghy, 1990, "State and Market"; White, 1990a, "Implementing Reforms."

32. Kahler, 1990, "Orthodoxy."

33. J. Nelson, 1989, "Long-Haul Economic Reform," 18–19.

34. J. Nelson, 1989, "Long-Haul Economic Reform," 20; Whitehead, 1989, "Democratization."

35. Callaghy, 1990, "State and Market."

36. See also comments by Helleiner, 1986b, "Policy-Based Program Lending," 61.

37. Lancaster, 1988, "Political Economy."

38. Brinkerhoff and Morgan, 1989, "Structural Adjustment," point to a growing interdependence between lenders and donors. Debtors need external resources and donors need to "keep lending in order to protect the performance of loans outstanding."

39. Nicholas, 1988, *World Bank's Lending,* 4.

40. Green and Allison, 1986, "World Bank's Agenda," 63. See also White, 1990b, "Policy Reforms."

41. Lindenberg, 1989, "Economic Adjustment," 387.

42. J. Nelson, 1989, "Long-Haul Economic Reform," 22.

43. Kahler, 1989, "International Financial Institutions"; Helleiner, 1986b, "Policy-Based Program Lending," 61.

44. J. Nelson, 1989, "Long-Haul Economic Reform," 20.

45. Mosley, 1986, "Agricultural Performance," 524–525.

46. DPMC, 1987, "Sustainability," 28. See also Brinkerhoff and Ingle, 1989, "Structured Flexibility."

47. Larry Graham, for example, notes how donors have enabled technocrats to play a dominant role in the Mexican government. Remarks at a colloquium, December 1987, National Association of Schools of Public Affairs and Administration.

3

A Strategic Process
for Implementing Change

MODELS FOR IMPROVING IMPLEMENTATION

Clearly it makes a difference how policy reforms are implemented. Traditionally, those working in the field of development administration defined implementation as a problem in organizational capacity. From this perspective they recommended training, technical assistance, and structural changes such as decentralization. The development community has since begun to redefine implementation. Instead of emphasizing capacity in and of itself, people are asking, "What kind of capacity is needed to stimulate economic development in a particular setting?" This more pragmatic formulation defines capacity for implementation in terms of how well units perform. Instead of stating a priori what capacities, strategies, or structures are needed, it asks how to accomplish an intended result.[1] This approach to implementation is particularly appropriate for policy reforms, since many reforms challenge traditional views of capacity.

There are several versions of a performance-oriented approach. This chapter compares several that have been particularly influential in understanding development activities and considers how useful they are for policy reforms. They include public choice theory, contingency theory, management science, incrementalism, and social learning theory.

Public choice theory evaluates implementation according to how efficiently services are provided and how well they reflect individual preferences. The theory compares rules or institutions for determining what it is that people want and for translating preferences into collective choices. It assumes that individuals pursue their economic self-interest in the political arena just as they do in the marketplace. This assumption allows one to predict how individuals will behave under different institutional rules and for different policy issues. One then looks for institutions that encourage efficiency and responsiveness.

The theory predicts that officials working in public institutions have little incentive to be efficient. Not only are their budgets loosely related to their performance, it is difficult to measure and monitor results. In addition, policymaking and implementation are subject to transaction costs. It costs time and energy to make decisions and deliver services, costs that increase with the number of people who are involved.[2] Policies implemented through private or decentralized or competitive institutions are more apt to be responsive to particular preferences and more apt to be efficient. Even if governments decide to make services available and fund them, they can still turn to other, usually smaller, units to produce them. Marketlike exchanges also reduce corruption since they make it more difficult for public officials to create artificially scarce goods by curtailing their supply (rationing import licenses for example) and charging rents (or inflated payments).[3]

Elinor Ostrom and her associates have applied the theory to policies to improve rural infrastructure. For example, they observe that it is difficult to develop adequate roads in rural areas. Resources are scarce and roads are difficult to maintain. According to the theory, implementing road systems depends on two kinds of institutional incentives: to generate resources and to encourage their maintenance. An appropriate institution would inform beneficiaries about the benefits they will receive, require them to contribute resources of their own, commit them to maintain the facility over time, and allow them to participate in designing and monitoring the system. They review case studies of infrastructure in LDCs and conclude that "where the economic incentives are sufficiently strong, relatively small groups of users are capable of ensuring that road maintenance is performed."[4]

The theory has stimulated some of the more innovative thinking about LDC institutions. It has proved to be particularly provocative in emphasizing the importance of analyzing institutions and in proposing a theory for comparing institutional alternatives. In general, it recommends institutions that are decentralized and that provide voluntary, communal alternatives to centralized public authority. It is also useful in urging that those who benefit from policies should assume some responsibility for them.

Public choice is inadequate as the sole guide for designing institutions, however. It assumes that people have fixed preferences and that they are governed primarily by economic self-interest, despite evidence that preferences change and that people respond to a number of different sentiments.[5] It also assumes that competition is sufficient to hold separate organizations in check, and it thereby underestimates the power of elites and structural conditions in a society. Its predetermined body of theory and single criterion of efficiency limits the kinds of concerns that individuals take into account in making institutional choices.

Contingency theory, highly influential within organization studies, is a second pragmatic approach to implementation. It urges that an organization's structures should be matched to the type of task it performs and to the pressures in its environment.[6] Samuel Paul has been particularly creative in applying contingency theory to LDC settings. Most development tasks, he urges, are characterized by uncertainty about the best way to proceed, and are carried out in a rapidly changing and often nonsupportive setting. To match these characteristics, managers have to be flexible and adapt their organizations to their tasks and settings.[7]

Contingency theory is useful because it emphasizes the context in which development changes are carried out. It also appreciates that policies require appropriate arrangements rather than a single organizational solution for all situations. It offers valuable insights into the kinds of organizations that are fitting to specific policy changes. Nevertheless, contingency theory is an incomplete guide to implementing policy changes. It relies on very general directions such as telling managers to be more flexible when their policies are complex and their settings are uncertain.[8] It is not based on a theory of behavior that explains why people would adopt their tasks and organizations to the setting. Finally, because contingency theory emphasizes adaptation, it is not so useful in changing a situation. (The approach proposed in this study draws on contingency theory but relies on an enquiry process rather than a prescriptive theory to determine the "contingencies.")

Management science offers a third approach, sometimes pejoratively referred to as "blueprint management." It prescribes rational analysis to set goals and establish clear guidelines and then relies on management to hold members accountable to these goals. "As its name implies, it suggests management by a preconceived, ordered plan. Borrowed from the world of engineering, it is an approach that defines a problem, cites objectives, chooses solutions, puts together resources, implements the plan and evaluates the results. It is hierarchical in structure and works from the 'top down.'"[9] For some, scientific management is particularly relevant to the structural adjustment process because of its emphasis on setting clear objectives and monitoring performance. It is implicit in many Bank studies of central ministries of finance and planning. These generally attempt to strengthen the capacity of central ministries to design rational policies and monitor whether ministries carry out the policies.[10]

This approach is too readily dismissed as inferior to more participatory approaches. Managers clearly need more technical skills, and organizations need more rational procedures, both of which are associated with this approach.[11] The approach also appreciates that strategic goals and objectives can be used to generate change in a system. At the same time, Brinkerhoff is right when he warns against a "management fix" to replace the earlier search for a "technical fix."[12]

An analysis of reform efforts in the Ministry of Rural Development (MDR) in Guinea illustrates the kinds of problems raised by scientific management approaches. The report reviewed a donor-funded study of the MDR and criticized its emphasis on rigorous analysis in central ministries at the expense of improvements in the operational capacity of program ministries. The donor study adopted a rational approach to analysis and management and defined capacity building as top-down control. In doing so, it ignored interaction, feedback, and adaptation throughout the system. Monitoring, for example, meant gathering predefined data rather than learning about policy results. As a result, the report concluded that the donor study offered little help in making ongoing adjustments.[13]

A variation on this approach comes out of the implementation literature. Because programs are seldom carried out as they were intended, the planning process should anticipate implementation problems. Since it is hard to change organizational behavior, designers should plan on modest changes; reorganizations and the number of actors should be kept as simple as possible; implementation problems should be anticipated from the outset; and implementation should be given over to those who are sympathetic towards the policy goals.[14] This model has been adopted in much of the literature on managing development activities. Arturo Israel, for example, urges that the evident weaknesses in LDC bureaucracies and the enormity of the development task make it important to keep tasks as simple and focused as possible and to set clear objectives.[15]

A rather different approach prescribes incremental adjustments to existing policies. Based on a widely respected body of theory, incrementalism predicts that individuals and organizations tend to continue what they are presently doing with only small adjustments. Instead of driving the process, goals often emerge during the implementation process. Moreover, these observers add, incremental adjustments not only describe what exists in reality, but marginal changes are the best way to carry out policy since larger changes may only make matters worse.[16] Those in control, the presumed experts, too readily believe they have the answers. They are less apt to do irretrievable damage if they make small changes rather than large ones and look for chances to experiment, collect feedback, and make adjustments.[17]

There are problems in relying solely on an incremental approach to carry out policy reforms, however. First, financial problems in LDCs are critical and immediate, and incremental adjustments are unlikely to deal with the severity of the problems. Second, incremental adjustments made during periods of financial crises may only make things worse. Charles Levine reports a piece of evidence based on a study of police departments in the United States facing financial crisis. Officials responded with across-the-board incremental adjustments such as deferring maintenance or freezing operating expenses. These actions only made things worse in the long run, however. The reductions eroded the quality of the workforce, avoided difficult choices, and paralyzed decisionmaking.[18]

Social learning theory offers yet another approach to implementation. It begins with a normative statement that development should enable all members of a society to make choices about their futures. Implementation, therefore, has to engage implementors and beneficiaries alike in a planning and monitoring process.[19] It is also important to mobilize local communities to generate "social energy" and enable people to have greater influence over their lives.[20] The social learning model is similar to public choice theory in two respects. It assigns responsibility for policies to those who have the greatest interest in seeing that they are carried out, and it is suspicious of bureaucrats who are not closely linked to local communities. Their methodologies are significantly at odds, however. Whereas public choice theory relies on a limited set of assumptions about behavior in order to develop a predictive theory, social learning theory is more interested in stimulating new behavior to emerge in a situation. It has been particularly appealing to voluntary organizations in developing a strategy for promoting small-scale development activities at local levels.[21]

A PROCESS APPROACH FOR
DESIGNING AND EFFECTING CHANGE

To summarize the argument thus far: Developing countries are facing critical financial problems and experiencing severe economic decline. Policy reforms to liberalize economies have been proposed and in some cases have been put in place. While results are uneven, many of the reforms are proving difficult to implement and sustain. Further, sustainable economic development requires supporting investments and new institutional arrangements, ones that will significantly change how activities are designed and carried out.

In the meantime, there is no general, prescriptive model that observers and practitioners can rely on, although several provide important insights. These include the prescription in public choice theory to diversify the institutions that provide services, and the argument based on contingency theory that strategies and organizational structures should be appropriate to one's task and situation. They include the prescription in management science for skilled analysis, the argument in implementation theory that goals can simplify and guide a complex process, the prescription from social learning theory that all those with an interest in a policy need to be involved in shaping it, and the observation from incrementalism that implementation proceeds best by adjustments and learning from experience.

Officials and practitioners continue to draw from a number of theories, and the development field has been unwilling to settle on any one of them. Increasingly, those involved in policy changes are adopting a *process approach* to plan and carry out policy changes. A process that directly involves interested parties has several advantages. It provides officials with an opportunity to draw from any of these implementation strategies and to select those that help them cope with their situations. It ensures that officials will assume responsibility for designing appropriate policy responses and implementation strategies. It provides a mechanism for collaborating with those who have pertinent information and those who can provide useful analytic and technical assistance.

Consider an example in which officials have to implement a policy towards parastatals. Citing widespread evidence of inefficiency, international organizations typically attach conditions to their loans, requiring officials to liquidate parastatals and turn them over to the private sector. According to John Nellis, however, it would be far better if advisers helped officials develop a process for deciding what to do with the parastatals. The process would provide an occasion for diagnosing the problems with particular parastatals. An effective process would enable them to examine the role of the parastatals in the local economy, to select which should be privatized, to market these, to handle sales or leases, and to ensure that credit is available to potential buyers. Such a process could also introduce the analytic tools from such approaches as public choice theory or management science as resources for officials.[22]

The lessons in Chapter 2 suggest that those involved in a process to design ways to implement policies need to do at least three things: generate new ideas, take the immediate context into account, and deal with the limitations and differences in views about economic development. Strategic analysis is a resource for designing a process that accomplishes these three tasks. It is a fairly common-sense technique for instituting change by diagnosing problems and developing a way to cope with them. As used here, it is a broadly conceived process that brings together a number of parties to assess the problems and opportunities in the immediate situation, set priorities, develop an appropriate policy, and design strategies to implement it.

Strategic management was developed in the United States, primarily for large private corporations.[23] It is often associated with sophisticated analysis and precise measurable objectives, and in this form it can easily overpower the capacity of many institutions. According to one study, local governments in the United States found it was either too difficult to carry out or the recommendations were sidetracked by bureaucrats reluctant to change.[24] Strategic implementation is used here in a more generic sense. It is not bound to a specific methodology but refers to an approach or way of thinking about designing and carrying out policies. The difference is captured in a definition by the International Labour Organisation. "Strategic management is not a privileged domain of the most advanced institutions nor is it a set of rigid rules: it is a concept, a state of mind, which can be applied in any environment and at any stage of development if the institution is prepared to tackle fundamental questions concerning its purpose, objectives, orientation, resources, competence, performance and effectiveness. If there is a determination to address these crucial issues, a convenient opportunity and way can always be found even in young and less-experienced institutions."[25]

Those involved in a strategic process diagnose the problems and opportunities in their environments and then identify a purpose and a strategy for achieving it. Strategic purpose as a concept is particularly appropriate for coping with severe economic problems. It was developed for situations where managers found that their environments were changing and complex and even hostile to their efforts. It assumes that those responsible should go on the offensive as it were, look for opportunities to be effective, and even influence their environment by strategically looking for opportunities to innovate.

Strategic thinking is appropriate where incremental adjustments are inadequate. The study of fiscal crises cited earlier found that in times of fiscal stress, marginal changes can create new problems. It distinguished among four kinds of situations according to how severe the crisis was and whether it was short- or long-range in nature. When crises were not too severe or were short-term, incremental management adjustments were possibly adequate. Where the fiscal problems were long-range and severe, as is true in LDCs, units found they had to make more drastic changes such as redefining their missions, reorganizing their internal structure, and finding new ways to deliver services.[26] It does not simply try to improve the capacity in the government. Indeed the task and situation may suggest it would be better to diversify tasks to other units and help to build their capacity instead.[27]

The version of strategic analysis proposed here, however, does borrow from incremental theory. In some cases it makes sense to establish clear goals and objectives. At other times participants will find it more useful to think of broader visions and purposes and then explore ways to achieve these. Often "a good policy idea is the *result* of a stream of experience, not the starting point. . . . *Because* we cannot know the results of our ideas, we need to try them out in action and learn from experience; based on that learning, we may need to modify not only our actions but also the policy idea and the original objectives."[28] Participants may begin with a strategic purpose rather than a well-defined policy and then "manage by groping along." According to Robert Behn, "an excellent manager has a very good sense of his objectives but lacks a precise idea about how to realize them. . . . Despite years of experience and study, even the best manager must grope along. He tests different ideas and gauges their results. Then he tries different combinations and permutations of the more productive ideas."[29] In this way, a strategic purpose is combined with experimenting and adjusting.

Strategic processes challenge a vast literature that documents the difficulty of bringing about change, particularly in situations that are starved for resources and riddled with corruption. It also counters many who say that significant change in any organization is virtually impossible, that responsible parties are more apt to be self-servers than problem-solvers. Although the implementation problems discussed earlier confirm that individuals are loathe to change, there is a growing accumulation of cases where individuals, particularly in crisis-ridden settings, have systematically tried to bring about change. This study is grounded in these actual efforts and is addressed to those who are trying to introduce new ideas and approaches.

A FRAMEWORK FOR A STRATEGIC PROCESS

There are two ways to design a strategic approach to policy design and implementation. One stresses team building, workshops, consultations, and consensus building. It incorporates a broad array of knowledge and sentiment and motivates those who will be carrying out the plans by involving them in designing strategies.[30] A second approach pays more attention to the cognitive aspects of the strategic planning process and prescribes structured techniques to bring participants together to consider their options.

Strategic management processes in LDCs have drawn more from the first emphasis. Given the low level of commitment and skills among officials in many of these situations, it is natural that proponents would focus on teamwork and consensus building among participants. There are some limitations with this emphasis, however. It neglects the importance of information and the need for new ideas. Chris Argyris, a major proponent of teamwork and human development within organizations, acknowledges that too frequently the consensus-building approach neglects the cognitive dimensions of decisionmaking. He proposes a more conscious effort to draw from both approaches simultaneously.[31]

The proposed strategic process follows Argyris's advice to take both participation and cognitive processes seriously. It particularly stresses the cognitive elements, the need to collect more information and explore new models, since these have been relatively neglected in studies to date. Part Two of this book describes how to carry out a strategic process. It is based on a framework that is designed to avoid some of the problems that can arise in carrying out a process approach.

First, it is easy for planning processes to be dominated by external consultants. Many of the cases that describe strategic approaches depend almost wholly on the initiatives of external, trained consultants. Outside experts with process skills can be important resources. They bring a fresh perspective and expertise; they have a repertoire of skills to stimulate interaction and discussion; and they are less apt to have a vested interest in existing procedures or activities. There is a danger, however, that consultants may create a dependency among local officials and may unduly mystify the process. There is also a tendency in these situations for the procedures to become more important than the substance of the plans. These problems are particularly troubling in the LDC context, where consultants are readily identified with the external organizations that are promoting difficult and unwanted policy changes.

The framework makes the logic of the process available to all participants. There is nothing obscure or particularly sophisticated about the steps. Most are based on common sense and managers may find they already engage in strategic analysis on their own. A framework demystifies that process and involves local officials as early as possible. A number of frameworks have been proposed for LDCs and this framework draws from these. It tries to avoid the specialized language often associated with process models. The framework describes what is involved, helps officials identify elements that are particularly relevant to them, and gives them more ownership of the process. It allows them to determine where external consultants will be useful, identify the skills they need, and negotiate more effectively with outsiders for particular skills.

A second problem can arise with process approaches. There is a tendency to care more about reaching a consensus than about debating issues or learning new information. A typical process, for example, asks managers to diagnose their situation and relies on a series of group process techniques to carry out the diagnosis. According to one highly regarded manual, a process approach "assumes that most of the information the participants need to solve the issue at hand already exists somewhere within the group."[32] This assumption, however, unduly limits the kinds of solutions that a group will consider. It is inappropriate for policy reforms, many of which involve significant innovations and require new ways of thinking about issues. While facilitators can, and undoubtedly do, interject new information and new perspectives, a consensus approach tends not to emphasize new ideas.

It is well known that individuals have a hard time looking at their work critically and questioning the validity of what they are doing. Organization members prefer to stay with comfortable routines and make incremental changes. Chris Argyris makes a telling distinction between single-loop and double-loop learning. Single-loop learning consists of incremental adjustments to events. Double-loop learning, by contrast, involves reviewing one's purposes and operating assumptions. Changes in these are much more difficult and, in fact, are unlikely unless there is some external point of reference.[33]

A framework provides such an external reference by laying out the kinds of issues and questions that participants need to ask. The proposed framework draws on the numerous case studies and substantive research that are relevant to implementing policy reforms. Examples include studies on decentralization, financial management, organizational incentives, and community development. The analytic and prescriptive models cited earlier, including public choice, contingency theory, and management science also offer useful insights. By including analytic categories that reflect current research on implementation and policy changes, the framework encourages participants to examine recent studies, to define what new information they need, and to process the information they already possess.

A third problem with process approaches is their dependence on the interest and commitment of senior officials. LDC officials are noted for being insecure and lacking creativity, and bureaucracies are well known as arenas where red tape controls events. Unfortunately, there is no agreed-on theory stating when officials will be willing to realistically diagnose their situations or develop creative strategies to implement policy changes. Much of the existing theory about organizational behavior, in fact, predicts quite the opposite, that bureaucrats will inevitably be caught up in consuming turf battles and protective power plays.

The study and its proposed framework assume that there are some officials willing to take an innovative look at their activities and exercise some leadership in promoting such an analysis. It also assumes that officials are governed by a variety of motives. They may be so impressed by the problems they are confronting and by the "performance gaps" in their organizations that they will be open to exploring new approaches.[34] By enabling such officials to take ownership of the process, the framework can strengthen the hand of those who are willing to exercise some leadership. It is also worth recalling Michael Patton's rejoinder that one of the roles of consultants is to look for opportunities to stimulate others to take initiatives.[35]

Finally, a framework encourages cumulative learning. Case studies are typically used to conduct research on implementation because they take particular situations and processes into account. It is difficult, however, to deduce more general conclusions from cases. A common framework makes it possible for observers to ask comparable questions and explore similar hypotheses. The present study tries to systematize the assumptions in recent efforts to promote strategic analysis and encourage more research and systematic comparison.

The framework is just that. It can be amended and adapted to specific cases to help officials take the problems in Chapter 1 and the lessons in Chapter 2 into account. There is a remaining problem, however. Is it realistic to assume that those concerned with policy questions are willing to participate in a learning process and to learn from experience and from dialogues and collaboration? Does the framework overestimate the willingness of officials to promote change? The next chapter examines the realism of relying on a collaborative and strategic process to develop strategies for change.

NOTES

1. The Performance Management Project, funded by USAID, has been an important stimulus. See Rondinelli, 1987, *Development Administration;* and Brinkerhoff, 1990, *Improving Performance.*

2. Buchanan and Tullock, 1962, *Calculus.*

3. Krueger, 1979, "Political Economy"; Nicholson and Connerley, 1989, "Impending Crisis"; Ostrom, et al., 1988, *Rethinking Institutional Analysis.*

4. Ostrom, et al., 1990, *Institutional Incentives,* 22.

5. According to March and Olsen, 1989, *Rediscovering Institutions,* 130, "subjectively experienced political interests tend to be inconsistent, unstable, and endogenous." Aggregative theories also ignore "the ways in which the political system itself contributes to the creation and elaboration of citizen interests."

6. Hage and Finsterbusch, 1987, *Organizational Change;* Rondinelli; Middleton and Verspoor, 1990, *Planning Education Reforms;* Brinkerhoff, 1990, *Improving Performance.*

7. Paul, 1982, *Managing Development.*

8. White, 1987, *Creating Opportunities,* 225–227.

9. Dichter, 1987, *Development Management,* 3.

10. Lamb, 1986, *Institutional Dimensions.*

11. Dichter, 1987, *Development Management.*

12. Brinkerhoff, 1988, "Implementing Integrated Rural Development."

13. Diallo, et al., 1988, "Organization Development." For critiques of management science approaches, see also L. White, 1990a, "Implementing Reforms"; Saasa, 1985, "Public Policy-Making"; and Sanwal, 1988, "Designing Training."

14. O'Toole, 1986, "Policy Recommendations," 200; Bardach, 1977, *Implementation Game.*

15. Israel, 1987, *Institutional Development;* Brinkerhoff and Ingle, 1989, "Structured Flexibility."

16. Lindblom, 1959, "Muddling Through."

17. Nelson and Winter, 1982, *Evolutionary Theory.*

18. Levine, 1985, "Police Management," 692.

19. Korten, 1980, "Community Organization"; Uphoff, 1985, "Gal Oya."

20. Hirschman, 1988, "Social Energy"; Uphoff, 1985, "Gal Oya"; Uphoff, 1986, *Local Institutional Development.*

21. Korten, 1987, "NGO Strategies"; Huntington, 1987, *Accelerating Institutional Development.*

22. Nellis, 1986, *Public Enterprises.* See also Shirley, 1988, "The Experience with Privatization."

23. Hammermesh, 1983, *Strategic Management.*

24. Bryson and Roering, 1988, "Initiation of Strategic Planning."

25. Kubr, 1982, *A Management Development Institution,* 3.

26. Levine, 1985, "Police Management," 691–695.

27. Brinkerhoff and Ingle, 1989, "Structured Flexibility."

28. Golden, 1989, "Innovation," 9–10. Compare Korten, 1984, "Strategic Organization," in which he compares strategic planning, management, and organizations and argues strongly for the last alternative.

29. Behn, 1988, "Management by Groping Along," 645.

30. Eadie and Steinbacher, 1985, "Strategic Agenda Management."

31. Argyris, 1973, "Some Limits."

32. Silverman et al., 1986, *Action-Planning Workshops*, 5.

33. Argyris, 1977, "Double Loop Learning." Lindenberg and Crosby, 1981, *Managing Development*, also stress the value of a framework to encourage systematic reflection about one's situation.

34. Hage and Finsterbush, 1987, *Organizational Change*.

35. Patton, 1986, *Utilization-Focused Evaluation*.

4

A Model of
Interactive Policy Inquiry

Designing and implementing policy reforms and supporting actions is difficult. Experiences suggest that they are more apt to be successful if relevant parties collaborate in designing them, both to apply contextual knowledge and to explore alternative views. Chapter 3 proposed a collaborative process based on strategic thinking for designing and implementing changes. The concept of being strategic means that participants are doing more than learning from their experiences. They also need to be purposive. A similar emphasis on the value of being strategic as opposed to simply learning from experience was made in a study of technological development in the NICs: "The acquisition of technological capability does not come merely from experience, though experience is important. It comes from conscious efforts—to monitor what is being done, to try new things, to keep track of developments throughout the world, to accumulate added skills, and to increase the ability to respond to new pressures and opportunities."[1]

This emphasis on a collaborative and strategic process poses a major question, however. Is it realistic to expect that collaboration is compatible with strategic and innovative thinking? The question is important since the two dominant models of the policy process place very little emphasis on interaction and learning. The technocratic version views policy design as the work of experts who search for certain and objective knowledge. The political version assumes that individuals pursue specific political and economic interests, and that policies result from bargaining and compromise among them, rather than from the exchange of ideas or learning from innovations.

This chapter examines the assumptions in a collaborative process for designing and implementing change—assumptions about the role of expertise, the nature of knowledge, and the process of decisionmaking. They differ significantly from the assumptions made by technocratic and political models. As noted earlier, international economic institutions are taking dialogues and contextual information more seriously. They need, however, to examine their assumptions about decisionmaking, expertise, and the policy process.

Otherwise, the dialogues will remain very tenuous affairs, dominated by outsiders, resented by country officials, and limited in their appropriateness. After analyzing the assumptions in a collaborative approach to policymaking, this chapter proposes a model of interactive policy design and links it to strategic thinking.

ASSUMPTIONS IN A STRATEGIC APPROACH
TO POLICY DESIGN AND IMPLEMENTATION

Individual Rationality

Prevailing models of individual behavior reflect the heavy influence of economic models. One version, political economy, assumes that individuals and groups rationally pursue their self-interest, generally defined as economic interest. The technocratic version of economic analysis assumes that individuals, particularly when they have the training to use analytic techniques, can carrying out rational and relatively comprehensive analysis.

Cognitive models of behavior offer an alternative to these economic approaches. Individuals are assumed to be intendedly rational, that is, they have a capacity for rational thought, but their rationality is limited, or, in Herbert Simon's terms, *bounded*. Both of these points are important—the premise that individuals use their reason and are able to respond to ideas and learn from their experiences and also the premise that their reasoning powers are limited. There are several implications relevant to policy inquiry.[2]

First, individuals can be reached through ideas and persuasion as well as through economic and political incentives. Although individuals generally pursue their perceived interests, their definition of what is in their interest can evolve and change as they acquire more information or have more experiences.[3] Unlike economists, cognitive theorists cannot predict how individuals define their interests ahead of time. They assume, however, that it is more useful to understand how people come to define their interests and goals, why they behave as they do, what their preferences and goals are, and on what basis they change their views. They are willing to give up the simple, predictive model of the economists in order to gain a more realistic appreciation of the variety of motives and understandings that influence behavior. In Simon's words, "the study of the mechanisms of attention direction, situation defining, and evoking are among the most promising targets of political research."[4]

These cognitive limitations make it necessary to rely on the expertise and knowledge of stakeholders throughout a policy community.[5] It is especially useful to include those who experience policy firsthand. Experts can correct for their bounded rationality by including different views, consulting with and involving those who will be using and adapting the information from the outset.[6]

Second, individuals are influenced by their place in an organization and the expectations of others around them. According to March and Olsen, individuals are intentional, but not necessarily willful in an economic sense. Instead of being motivated by the anticipated consequences of their actions, they look for cues in their situation or from their position in an organization. Instead of always pursuing a rationally defined self-interest, they want to do what is appropriate and fitting. This assumption is very important for decisionmaking.[7] It means that institutions and policy decision procedures can have an influence on how people behave.

Simon makes a related point in predicting that individuals *satisfice* rather than maximize their goals and interests. Because an individual's capacity for selecting rational strategies is limited, there is a tendency to select satisfactory responses. Cognitive rationality predicts that individuals will select actions appropriate to their situations. As "satisficers," they usually do not look for the most efficient way to operate.[8]

This assumption makes a difference in organizations. According to Hirschman, there is a lot of *slack* in most organizations, and managers are willing to get along at a far less than optimal level. Whereas economists value competition because it enforces responsiveness, Hirschman finds that managers may actually be pleased when dissatisfied customers exit—it simply means the troublemakers are gone. Instead of changing to improve their efficiency, organizations are apt to accept a certain amount of slack and continue with business as usual. Competition, therefore, is not necessarily the best way to enhance efficiency. Improving procedures for gathering and handling information may be a better strategy.[9]

There are other limits on rationality that have an influence on decisionmaking. In a debate with Simon, Chris Argyris asked a revealing question: Why do individuals often oppose a new management information system (MIS)? According to Simon's cognitive model, individuals would adopt an MIS if it helped them analyze and use information. Argyris, however, suggests that their feelings would also influence how they reacted. "Managers may fight the MIS, especially when they are effective in helping them to achieve their objectives, because the use of the system reduces the role of their intuition, reduces their space of free movement, increases their experience of psychological failure." He adds that this emphasis on feelings does not deny the intended rationality of individuals; it only suggests that a fuller model of behavior is needed, one that acknowledges "man, as a person who feels; experiences chaos; manifests spontaneity; becomes turned-on without planning it or being able to explain it in terms of consistency of conscious purpose; thinks divergently; and who may strive, at times, to separate himself from his past."[10]

These assumptions portray a considerably different person than is implied by economic models of decisionmaking. People are intentional and responsive to ideas and willing to listen to reasons that people give for different policies. However, they neither rationally sort out their self-interests nor single-mindedly pursue them. They respond to cues from their situation about what is appropriate, and they are willing to accept reasonable and satisfactory solutions and decisions rather than calculate the best strategy to achieve a certain goal.

The Nature of Policy Inquiry

Much of the policy reform debate assumes that analysis is a rational and comprehensive effort to find the "truth" or the optimal solution. Experts define problems, gather evidence, and, using accepted methodologies, arrive at an objectively valid policy response.[11] An alternative approach, and one that is more consistent with the above discussion of limitations on rationality, describes analysis as a process of *policy inquiry* rather than objective truth seeking. According to Bozeman, policy analysts are more apt to select policies according to their credibility than their truth. "The basic notion behind the credibility model is that the justification of propositions is not dependent on consistency with empirically tested models or with any other concept of truth, but with the subjective believability of propositions." Credibility models turn on the kinds of arguments one uses to make a case. They recognize that decisionmakers often rely on their experience, intuition, and judgment and that these are more appropriate to the policy arena where one is usually working with local effects, with a small "N," and where rules of generalizability do not apply.[12]

Policy inquiry is realistic about the uncertain and tentative nature of policy knowledge and assumes there may be a variety of legitimate views on policy strategies. Even those who agree on economic growth as a goal or on market arrangements as a strategy, for example, are likely to differ on what these mean in practice. Policy analysis, therefore, becomes an interactive process of inquiry among experts and interested parties. It assumes that policy dialogues provide an occasion for exploring and discussing options.

Policy inquiry adopts the cognitive assumption that although individuals often act out of self-interest, they can reason together about experiences and often will change how they define their self-interest. In one description, political leaders "are purposive, but they operate in an uncertain world with incomplete information, they don't search for alternatives very systematically, and they do a lot of satisficing rather than maximizing."[13] Policy inquiry allows the parties to give reasons for their positions, identify what information would be most useful to them, and test their assumptions against others' views.

Policy inquiry fits with an integrative approach to policymaking. March and Olsen distinguish between two views of the policy process. An aggregative approach, associated with political economy and pluralism, assumes that policies emerge from a political process, the purpose of which is to aggregate different interests into a set of policies. An integrative approach is quite different. Policies reflect an effort to find a common meaning in a community. "In an integrative process, the will of the people is discovered through deliberation by reasoning citizens and rulers seeking to find the general welfare within a context of shared social values."[14] There is an interesting similarity between this view and the analysis of the NICs presented earlier. Recent studies of the NICs argue that an important reason for their high growth rates has been a strong commitment by the government and people to economic development and a willingness to make some sacrifices to achieve that.[15]

A policy inquiry approach also fits with research on the utilization of policy research. Studies confirm that the specific recommendations of policy analysts and researchers are often not used. The same studies go on to show that even if recommendations are not adopted, the supporting analysis may still prove useful if it helps policymakers clarify their thoughts and consider alternatives. Weiss refers to the "enlightenment function" of policy research and analysis. She adds that this function is most likely when a long time frame is adopted, because enlightenment takes time and therefore studies that look for opinion change immediately are less likely to find it.[16] Joan Nelson makes a similar observation about policy reforms. She suggests that many of the studies that have been done within Kenya and Zambia, for example, "may produce their main results indirectly and after some years' lag—by influencing the outlook of younger Kenyan and Zambia officials, academics and politicians."[17]

Policy inquiry thus engages participants in a common discussion. It also brings together individuals with different views and experiences and introduces what the economist F. W. Hayek refers to as "time and place information." Hayek distinguishes between models that are generalizable and those that refer to specific contexts. Although both are necessary in any policy decision, contextual information, with all of its scientific limitations, is particularly important. It refers to "a body of very important but unorganized knowledge which cannot possibly be called scientific in the sense of knowledge of general rules—the knowledge of the particular circumstances of time and place. It is with respect to this that practically every individual has some advantage over all others in that he possesses unique information of which beneficial use might be made."[18] Because they possess "time and place" information, individuals have different understandings of policy objectives and the causal relations among events. These different views need to become part of the inquiry process.

Policy Inquiry and Political Reality

The stress on the potential of policy inquiry does not deny the reality of political motivations. Leaders obviously pay close attention to the political arena and will choose a package of reforms with this in mind. The model, however, does assume that the political arena itself is not fixed, that political leaders have some room for maneuver, for interpreting policies, for building coalitions, and for sequencing reforms. An effective policy inquiry process would deal with these issues, and would explore the views of different parties and opportunities for taking them into account.

Kohli's insightful study of the policy reform process in India illustrates the influence of political agendas on economic policy decisions. Politics even influenced decisions to establish a commission to review economic performance. "If one is not cautious, one could easily conclude that policy momentum in India is driven by the expert knowledge that is periodically brought to bear on pressing national problems. Such a conclusion would be misleading. The decision to set up commissions is a political decision. Commission members are appointed by leaders and the policy preferences of these members are generally well known. Most important, whether the government chooses to act on a report is a political decision." Kohli's further analysis, and his comparison of the policy responses of Indira and Rajiv Gandhi, underscore the importance of the political agenda and the skill with which Indira Gandhi, in particular, combined economic and political calculations. Indira was able to manage the tension between political and economic reforms by depoliticizing the decisions, by ensuring that changes were gradual, by diverting political attention to regional issues, and by relying on a broad political trust.[19]

The point is that officials have some autonomy and can often shape the way in which issues are posed. Even when political interests determine the policy agenda, policy elites determine the alternatives that are considered.[20] This reflective role of government is emphasized by Hugh Heclo: "Governments not only 'power' (or whatever the verb form of that approach might be); they also puzzle. Policy-making is a form of collective puzzlement on society's behalf; it entails both deciding and knowing. The process of making . . . policies has extended beyond deciding what 'wants' to accommodate, to include problems of knowing who might want something, what is wanted, what should be wanted, and how to turn even the most sweet-tempered general agreement into concrete collective action."[21]

Assumptions About Implementation

This emphasis on bounded rationality and policymaking as an inquiry process changes the nature of implementation. Implementors no longer carry out preformed mandates; instead they continue the inquiry process. Implementation emerged as an important issue in the United States in the 1960s and 1970s as governments adopted new social programs. Observers asked whether policies were carried out as intended and concluded that policy mandates were either drastically altered by unresponsive bureaucracies or redefined by special interests. As a result, those concerned with implementation looked for ways to hold officials accountable to the original policy designs and turned to evaluation and management controls.[22]

Views of implementation changed, however, as it became clearer that many policies were never "implementable" in the first place. Analysts, therefore, have to consider implementation, and the best way to do this is to think of analysis as a single, continuing process that includes decisionmakers, analysts, and managers. There are several reasons. First, responsible officials have firsthand, "time and place" knowledge about implementation problems that outsiders do not have. Second, unless officials have a sense of ownership of the implementation plan, they are unlikely to invest a great deal of energy in it. Third, long-lasting, sustainable changes are much more likely if officials have some discretion to make changes in the process of implementing policies. Instead of asking whether an organization has carried out a policy as intended, one asks whether those charged with carrying out the policy have successfully adjusted it to deal with the problems that arise.[23] Policies, in fact, may be purposefully ambiguous in order to gain more support and allow implementors room to explore areas of agreement. Problems that arise during implementation may simply reflect this ambiguity in policies and the fact that policies often evolve and take shape only as they are carried out.[24]

A MODEL OF THE POLICY INQUIRY PROCESS

According to these assumptions, individuals have limited cognitive abilities, but they can engage in reasoned exchanges or inquiry with others. They look for satisfactory or credible strategies on the basis of these exchanges. They engage in what Heclo calls "policy-oriented learning."[25] Is this a realistic view of the policy decision process? Do people actually change their views and learn from others and from experience?

A model of the policy decision process identifies the conditions for this kind of learning[26] (see Figure 4.1). On the left, the model differentiates between two aspects of the *policy environment*. There are given properties of the system, such as natural resources and cultural values, which remain reasonably stable. There are also external events, such as changes in technology, in political coalitions, in public opinion. Such events introduce change into the system.

Figure 4.1 A Model of Policy Learning

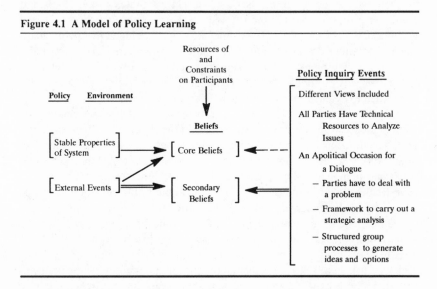

Individuals also hold two kinds of *beliefs*, which in part reflect their resources and constraints. One kind is called core beliefs. These include values such as social equity or full employment and also views on the scope of the government and the role of the market. There are also secondary beliefs; examples are views on whether to decentralize agricultural services, reorganize an agency, or remove subsidies. External events can influence secondary beliefs (the double arrow) and have some influence on core beliefs (the single arrow) even though the latter remain relatively stable. Reductions in commodity prices, severe economic crisis, or increases in inflation are events that can lead people to rethink their core values. An earlier chapter already noted that severe economic crises can produce changes in core beliefs as well as secondary ones.

Policy inquiry events are on the right side of the figure. The broken arrow suggests that policy inquiry may affect core values under certain conditions, and the double arrow indicates that it has a stronger influence on secondary views such as choices about institutions and implementation strategies. The extent to which the process can influence core values is worth exploring since much of the debate over policy reforms occurs at this level.

When core values conflict, "the tendency is for each coalition to talk past the other and thus for a 'dialogue of the deaf' to persist."[27] An example might be a deadlock on whether to encourage exports; such a move could offend those who value self-sufficiency and believe it is wrong to become too vulnerable to external commodity purchases.

Sabatier proposes that learning or change in core values can occur when three conditions are present: First, "both sides must have sufficient technical resources to be able to criticize the other's causal models and data. They must also have the incentive to expend scarce resources to engage in such an analytical debate." Second, and more important, there must be present "a relatively apolitical forum in which experts of the respective coalitions are forced to confront each other. . . . The purpose is to force debate among professionals from different belief systems in which their points of view must be aired before peers. . . . [The result is] a greater convergence of views over time concerning the nature of the problem and the consequences of various policy alternatives." Third, there must be good performance indicators and causal models.[28] An adaptation of these conditions is included in the right-hand column of Figure 4.1.

First, different views must be included. Deciding who should be involved at each stage becomes a critical part of the process. The policy literature refers to a policy subsystem, "those actors from a variety of public and private organizations who are actively concerned with a policy problem or issue."[29] Such a subsystem is still relatively undefined, however, and those involved still need to make a strategic decision about whom to include in each situation. As Chapter 2 noted, in some situations it is helpful to insulate decisionmakers from some political pressures. Deyo found that such insulation had fostered effective policymaking in the East Asian NICs. A major assumption in this study is that decisionmakers need to look for opportunities to connect their economic prescriptions with political realities. Although insulation may be a reasonable strategy, at some point political inquiry and inclusion need to be taken seriously. One way to do this is to include different political perspectives in the dialogues or decision process, either directly or perhaps informally.

Second, all parties need to have the resources to contribute to the analysis of the reforms. A review of policy dialogues conducted by USAID in the agriculture sector concluded that far more attention should be paid to improving the analytic capacity of LDCs to conduct background studies and make recommendations. This should include not only skills in using diagnostic tools such as sector assessments, but also analytic skills that allow them to examine the effects of current policies and likely effects of policy changes. They also need to be able to examine the "assumptions and conditions under which the recommended policies will serve the stated objectives and when not."[30]

Third, there needs to be an apolitical occasion for a dialogue and an opportunity to carry out a strategic analysis of a problem area. The use of the term "apolitical" needs to be clarified. On the one hand, Kahler is correct that the political content of the dialogues needs to be taken far more seriously than is usually the case. This does not mean that leaders are there solely to reflect the push of different interest groups in the society, however. It means that the dialogues have to include more than the technocratic core in a country. Political differences are real and need to be dealt with. But it is called "apolitical" because it is an occasion for policy inquiry about a problem situation rather than a traditional bargaining session among competing interests.[31]

The broken arrow in Figure 4.1 suggests that the influence of policy inquiry on core beliefs in particular is contingent on these conditions: relevant parties are included, all have technical resources for carrying out analysis, and there is an occasion for engaging in a dialogue and carrying out strategic analysis. The influence on secondary beliefs is usually stronger, hence the double arrow.

Inquiry can assume different forms—joint studies, briefings, high-level talks between lending agencies and governing officials, informal sessions with expert analysts, and forums that bring together several political groups. It is also helpful to think of a sequence of inquiry agendas—the initial framework for a policy change, alternative ways of defining an agreed-on policy goal, and implementation activities. The idea of a sequence is important. Kahler notes that a severe impediment on constructive policy reform dialogue is the sense of crisis that usually surrounds it. He recommends instead a practice of "continuous policy consultations," which would routinize and extend the dialogues. He continues, "overall, such discussions lengthen the 'shadow of the future'—the realization on the part of both [international organizations] and governments that they will confront one another in the context of such discussions at regular intervals. Crisis-determined lending, on the other hand, offers no such assurance."[32]

Policy inquiry can continue during implementation as parties discuss the implications of their efforts. Levine's research on cutback management, discussed earlier, found that as fiscal problems got worse, officials considered responses that they had earlier rejected. He also found that departments tended to develop capacity when they needed it, and that fiscal stress was an external event that forced a number of managers to consider doing something innovative. Those who handled fiscal problems the best were able to do two things: formulate and stick to a strategic plan and develop a climate that supported experimentation.[33] Similarly, Joan Nelson cites a number of countries where earlier failures with reforms were later followed by more successful efforts.[34]

CONCLUSIONS

The model predicts that policy inquiry can be structured to lead to innovative strategies. It assumes first that individuals do have a capacity for approaching problems rationally, but it is a limited capacity. In carefully designed situations they can learn from others and develop alternative views. Second, implementation strategies have to deal with a particular policy in a particular setting. It is important to get information from a number of those involved and to proceed incrementally, learning and adapting. Third, most sectoral policy changes involve a fairly complex set of actions and take place in difficult and politically charged surroundings. Those involved need to be strategic in their approach to implementation—assessing problems and opportunities and focusing on critical steps where they can have some influence. Fourth, bureaucratic energy and commitment to change are scarce resources, and Third World officials are typically not used to taking a strategic approach to implementation. One way to overcome these limitations is to include those actually responsible for implementation as part of the planning process. Involvement has two purposes: to gain their commitment to the plans that evolve and to make sure that the plans deal with the actual problems the implementors are likely to confront.

This approach to policy design and implementation is appropriate for the kinds of hybrid policy reforms described in Chapter 1. Table 1.2 emphasized the uncertainty surrounding policy changes and economic development, both intellectually and operationally. A process approach that emphasizes collaboration and learning fits with the lack of knowledge, the complexity, and the uncertainty associated with sectoral policy changes. It fits with policy changes for a second reason. Developing country officials often feel that the policies are imposed on them. The model emphasizes the need to include them as key players in the process of designing how the policies are to be implemented.

NOTES

1. Dahlman, et al., 1987, "Managing Technological Development," 759.

2. A recent discussion of bounded rationality is found in Simon, 1985, "Human Nature," in which he also compares cognitive and economic models.

3. This approach is supported by psychological theory that says that individuals often define their interests as they get involved in a situation; for example, see Bem, *Beliefs*, 1970.

4. Simon, 1985, "Human Nature," 303.

5. Landau, 1986, "Decision Strategies"; Healy, 1986, "Interpretive Policy"; Torgerson, 1986, "Between Knowledge."

6. Patton, 1986, *Utilization-Focused Evaluation;* Mitroff and Emshoff, 1979, "Strategic Assumption Making."

7. March and Olsen, 1989, *Rediscovering Institutions,* 160–161.

8. Simon, 1985, "Human Nature."

9. Hirschman, 1981, *Exit, Voice.*

10. Argyris, 1973, "Some Limits," 261, 263.

11. The same assumptions are true of donor-funded projects. Brinkerhoff and Ingle, "Structured Flexibility," 1989.

12. Bozeman and Landsbergen, 1989, "Truth and Credibility," 356, 365. Janis, 1989, *Crucial Decisions,* 149, concurs in urging policy decisions that are responsible and sensible rather than purportedly rational.

13. Kingdon, 1984, *Agendas,* 22.

14. March and Olsen, 1989, *Rediscovering Institutions,* 118.

15. Johnson, 1987, "Political Institutions"; Chu, 1989, "State Structure," for example.

16. Weiss, 1977, "Research"; Sabatier, 1988, "Advocacy Coalition," 131; Patton, 1986, *Utilization-Focused Evaluation.*

17. J. Nelson, 1984, "Political Economy," 989.

18. Hayek, 1945, "Use of Knowledge," 521.

19. Kohli, 1989, "Politics," 309–311.

20. Kingdon, 1984, *Agendas.*

21. Heclo, 1974, *Modern Social Policy,* 305.

22. Bardach, 1977, *Implementation Game;* Stone, 1980, "Implementation." For a review of the implementation literature from the perspective of development management, see Ingle, 1979, *Implementing.*

23. Patton, 1986, *Utilization-Focused Evaluation.*

24. Baier, et al., 1988, "Implementation," 161.

25. Heclo, 1974, *Modern Social Policy.* He defines policy as an "enduring alteration of thought," 306.

26. Sabatier, 1988, "Advocacy Coalition."

27. Sabatier, 1988, "Advocacy Coalition," 155.

28. Sabatier, 1988, "Advocacy Coalition," 155–156.

29. Sabatier, 1988, "Advocacy Coalition," 131.

30. Project Evaluation, The Agricultural Policy Analysis Project, December 1987, 11; Appendix 2, 4. Mimeo.

31. Kahler, 1989, "International Financial Institutions."

32. Kahler, 1989, "International Financial Institutions," 151–152.

33. Levine, 1985, "Police Management," 695–696.

34. J. Nelson, 1984, "Political Economy," 989.

5

Strategies for Conducting Policy Inquiry

CHARACTERISTICS OF A PROCESS FOR DESIGNING POLICY REFORMS

The model of policy learning developed in the preceding chapter (Figure 4.1), is appropriate for designing and enacting policy reforms in several respects. By including different views it assumes there is no single objective policy solution and that appropriate policies will come out of an interchange among these views. By requiring resources for good analysis it also assumes that policy formulation depends on more than an exchange of views, that it has to be based on good substantive studies. Finally, it assumes that dialogue will take place in some form—policy exchanges, formal and less formal planning sessions, and ongoing discussions during implementation. The dialogues are based on strategic analysis. They begin with a problem situation, diagnose the policy setting by reflecting on the nature of the problem, select major issues, and design strategies to cope with them. This chapter compares techniques for conducting the dialogues. In particular, it examines the rationale for the third element in the dialogues listed in Figure 4.1—structured group processes to generate ideas and options. The chapters in Part Two describe the process itself, including the application of these techniques to specific cases.

Constraints on Policy Inquiry

It is helpful to begin by considering why policy inquiry and learning are often problematic. Janis classifies the constraints into three categories: cognitive, affiliative, and egocentric.[1] Cognitive constraints are associated with bounded rationality and affect the process of analysis and inquiry. They include situational factors such as a short amount of time, limited resources and capacity for research and analysis, multiple tasks, the complexity of the problems, the lack of dependable knowledge, and ideological commitments. Simon adds an emphasis on the limited cognitive abilities of the individual "who is limited in computational capacity, and who searches very selectively through large realms of possibilities. . . . The search is incomplete, often inadequate, based on uncertain information and partial ignorance."[2] Research in design science confirms these limitations by showing that individuals can deal with only five to nine items at a time.[3]

Affiliative constraints refer to relations among participants. These include the need of individuals to maintain their power and status within an organization and their desire for compensation and social support. It also includes the need of members to have their proposals acceptable within the organization. These constraints make it likely that participants will not be innovative but will "play it safe" and develop plans designed to preserve consensus in the group. The third group, egocentric constraints, include "self-serving and emotive constraints" such as personal greed and desire for fame. Economists would remove the pejorative implication and predict that individuals pursue what is in their interest—their position in the organization, status, resources, and so forth. Again the problem is that these motives skew the analysis and design of policy strategies.

Criteria for Conducting Policy Inquiry

These constraints, when linked to the characteristics of reforms discussed in Chapters 1 and 2 and the propositions outlined in Chapters 3 and 4, suggest several criteria for conducting the process of inquiry.

First, different views on the nature of the problem need to be considered, views that reflect alternative assumptions about economic growth as well as Hayek's "time and place" information. A recent study by Kohli of policy reforms in India, where industrial growth has been very sluggish, illustrates the kind of fundamental disagreements about economic problems that are prevalent in LDCs. After noting that the Indian government is not objectively responding to an objective situation, he adds that Indian officials trace the country's economic problems to a variety of factors: inefficiency due to the state-controlled economy; low aggregate demand; and declining public investments. Differences at this basic level of explanation demonstrate significant disagreement and need to be reviewed during the policy inquiry process.[4]

Second, the process should generate new thinking and innovative ideas.[5] This criterion means that participants need to feel free to speculate about alternatives. They also need to be exposed to new ways of thinking about old issues and stimulated to approach problems in new ways. Traditional problem-solving techniques need to be supplemented with techniques for introducing new ideas and alternative perspectives. Participants need to be discouraged from moving to strategies or solutions too readily. They need time to reflect on and analyze their situation. They need to be stimulated to speculate about new approaches, and even new ways of thinking about old problems. Procedures for stimulating new ideas should protect against both groupthink and undue influence by a few participants. Research on small-group decisionmaking documents that both of these dynamics are widespread.[6]

Third, the process must enable participants to come to a decision—to identify priorities and strategies for implementing these priorities. Students of group processes conclude that we have learned how to analyze problems, but have less experience in synthesizing studies into a coherent decision. Since individuals cannot handle too much uncertainty, procedures and rules are needed to bring some order and coherence to the process, to organize the information, and enable participants to come to a decision.[7] In reflecting on his experiences with dialogue in Central America, Lindenberg notes that it was important to have clear rules, particularly when members of different political groups came together.[8]

Fourth, participants need to focus on the substance of the decisions and identify gaps in knowledge. Procedures must feed needed information into the decision process. Processes that focus on eliciting opinions and feelings may place less emphasis on substantive discussions. They may easily overlook the extent to which many decisions require new data and could benefit from substantive expertise.

Fifth, it is important to conduct the process in such a way that those involved feel committed to the proposed policy reforms and institutional changes. Research suggests that it may be difficult to arrive at decisions that are both technically sound and also supported by those who will be carrying them out. If one classifies decisions according to whether they are low or high on technical quality and whether or not they are acceptable, studies show that it is difficult to make decisions that rank high on both quality and acceptability. "If [the leader] attempts to achieve quality first, either through his own expertise or that of others, he must resort to an imposed solution and faces the real possibility of not being able to gain the necessary level of acceptance. Conversely, if he utilizes participation in order to gain acceptance, quality may not be achieved."[9] Observers agree that some level of commitment or sense of ownership is important if officials are going to carry out and continue the reforms. This criterion is especially relevant when country officials and representatives of lending agencies are both part of the discussions. In such cases it is important to ensure that external parties do not dominate the process because of their access to resources or technical skills.

Sixth, the process must recognize that individuals are not solely cognitive creatures but also have feelings and personal needs. Even if a new idea seems appealing, individuals may find it threatening and may reject it on those grounds. Thus the process needs to provide opportunities for people to express and reflect on such feelings. Some cohesion and trust among the participants is necessary if they are to question current practices and entertain new approaches.[10]

GROUP STRATEGIES

There are three different ways to approach group processes. This section compares them and suggests how well they meet the above criteria and deal with the constraints on inquiry.

Interpersonal Group Process

One cluster of techniques, often associated with organization development theory, emphasizes participation, inclusion in teams, and building of trust and consensus. Based on studies showing that members frequently stereotype each other and thus have difficulty communicating, the techniques emphasize interpersonal communication. In the context of policy decisions, teams are created to deal with specific problems and are asked to share perceptions and fears about policy goals and proposed changes. The approach assumes that individual commitment depends on being part of the process and on participating in establishing goals, objectives, and implementation plans. A review of research tested this assumption. It found that participation in decisions does enhance workers' commitment to their organization, and that this finding held up in both field research and laboratory studies. The results indicate, however, that participation in goal setting does not necessarily increase workers' commitment to specific goals, nor does it automatically increase organizational productivity.[11]

Discussions of strategic approaches frequently borrow from organization development or human relations techniques. David Korten, for example, argues that since strategies are grounded in the culture of an organization, individuals need to be involved in decisionmaking so that they have a chance to reflect on this culture and to learn new values and commitments.[12] Another study refers to a strategic approach as "a marriage of organizational development and strategic planning" and notes that "strategic management requires attention to the human dimension of organization" as well as to analytic planning techniques.[13]

Interpersonal group processes include the following components: all those with a stake in the project are involved in decisions and strategy sessions; work is best done through teams, which must include some members from top management; team sessions stress communication, clarification, and agreement on goals and objectives; teams focus on specific tasks.[14] The emphasis on work groups, in fact, has been very influential in much of the work on development management funded by USAID. It has also been endorsed by many within the World Bank as the preferred technology in working with LDC officials.[15]

The approach meets several of the criteria for effective policy inquiry. For example, participation enhances commitment to the choices that are made and it does take into account individuals' feelings and personal needs. On the other hand, the approach does not rate very high on generating innovative ideas. It tends to rely on information members of the group already have, and although it is possible to introduce new information, that has not been the emphasis. It also focuses on consensus building at the expense of introducing alternative ideas or dealing openly with conflict,[16] and can result in what Janis calls "groupthink." Group members "tend to evolve informal objectives to preserve friendly intragroup relations and this becomes part of the hidden agenda at their meetings."[17]

Interactive Approaches

These rely on interaction just as do the above. However, there is more emphasis on political exchanges—group discussion, bargaining, negotiation, and exchange—than on building interpersonal trust. Political interaction, conducted as relatively open discussions of policy issues, provides an occasion for persuading others, giving reasons for a position, and challenging others' views. It builds consensus by actually modifying ideas and viewpoints, rather than by looking either for commitment or for an underlying consensus in the group. These approaches do not necessarily generate new ideas, however. A strong personality can dominate the process, or a few individuals can sway the group based on their status or position. As with interpersonal groups, members can indulge in groupthink and come to support the dominant view without openly questioning it. Often ideas are evaluated prematurely before they are openly aired, and minority views are easily stifled.

Structured Group Processes

A third strategy places more emphasis on the cognitive elements in decision-making and on structuring the ways in which participants interact and deal with information. Often associated with strategic analysis, it structures decision processes to encourage creativity and avoid domination by a few individuals.[18] Essentially it separates the process of generating ideas from activities to evaluate those ideas and select among them. It thus tries to avoid any premature closure of ideas. The sequence encourages individuals to generate alternatives without being swayed by group sentiment or by a few dominant members. Individuals participate equally, ideas are taken on their merits, and there is less group conformity.[19]

Research on the process indicates that it does generate more creative thinking and new ideas, and that so-called "nominal groups have been found to be significantly superior to interacting groups in generating information relevant to a problem."[20] Mahler, however, raises questions about how well this approach meets the criterion of encouraging commitment. She compared a structured approach with a political interaction approach and found that the former did not foster greater participation as is often claimed. "When participation is measured as the perceived opportunity to express, even forcefully, reasons for believing in the worth of a proposal," a traditional interactive group was more participatory. She went on to echo concerns raised earlier in discussing policy inquiry, namely that it may not be wise to eliminate chances to persuade and influence people. Politics, after all, can "be a means to articulate or discover important values. Persuasion, as the first art of politics, can clarify as well as obscure interests, and bargaining is commonly effective as a means of resolving conflicts."[21]

It is possible to construct planning sessions that draw from two or more of these approaches according to the nature of the task and the makeup of the group. The following questions can be useful. Does the task require a cognitive approach and a search for new ideas? Is the problem a lack of trust or willingness to adopt new roles? Is the issue conflict ridden so that compromises and tradeoffs need to be encouraged? For example, one could adopt an interaction approach to provide an occasion for persuading others. One could also provide some structure to the process to ensure that a variety of ideas were explored and that none was able to foreclose discussion. And one could attend to the interpersonal aspects of the exchange and encourage individuals to express their feelings and fears and thus build some trust among stakeholders and commitment to the choice.

Table 5.1 indicates how each of the strategies logically deals with the criteria laid out earlier.

Table 5.1 Group Strategies and Policy Inquiry

| | Group Processes | | |
Criteria for Inquiry	INTERPERSONAL	INTERACTIVE	STRUCTURED
Elicit Alternative Views	1	2	3
Generate New Ideas	1	2	3
Arrive at a Choice[a]	3	3	3
Deal with Substance	1	2	3
Develop Commitment	2	3	1
Recognize Feelings	3	2	1

Note: Strategies are ranked from 1 to 3, from low to high. Approximate rankings based on general conclusions in the literature.

[a]All are ranked high on arriving at a choice, but the nature of the choice varies. Respectively: chosen consensus, agreement, underlying consensus.

COGNITIVE TECHNIQUES

The theory and process of policy inquiry tries to improve the quality of discussion by introducing substantive information into the decision process. The criteria outlined at the beginning of this chapter also stress the importance of new ideas and concepts and the need to counter the inevitable tendency to play it safe and indulge in groupthink. The remainder of this chapter introduces very briefly a number of techniques that stress cognition, concepts and reflection. Most are described in a very useful collection of techniques, entitled *Systems Tools for Project Planning*, published by the Agency for International Development.[22]

Improve Individual Thinking

Brainstorming. Brainstorming is a technique used by individuals or groups to generate multiple ways to conceptualize a problem. It can be incorporated into a structured process (see the nominal process below) or it can be conducted in a less structured manner as an interactive strategy. Brainstorming separates the process of generating new ideas from the process of evaluating them. If those processes are not separated, it is too easy to criticize ideas that at first seem unusual but that might lead to new perspectives on old problems if they were thought about for a while. Members are given a specific problem or question. They are then encouraged to present a wide variety of perspectives and ideas, taking turns to ensure that everyone has a chance. There are no correct ideas, and novel points of view are encouraged.[23] The strategy is especially useful in drawing out people with different expertise and experience, although one study found that the effectiveness of a brainstorming session is higher when people know each other and are motivated to solve the problem being discussed.[24]

Conceptualizing. Concepts can generate creativity by challenging people to look at events in new ways. People often need to "let go" of old ways of looking at a problem before they can use new ones. Forcing people to use and think about different concepts can encourage such "letting go" as well as "seeing new things." Michael Patton observes that, "concepts channel thought. Concepts order the world, telling us what things go together and what things are distinct from each other." The challenge, he continues, "is to know when a new situation can be appropriately handled by prior conceptualizations and when to resist imposing order through familiar concepts while taking the time to look for patterns unique to the circumstances at hand, circumstances that may require some new conceptualization."[25]

Patton illustrates the power of concepts by contrasting needs and assets, concepts particularly relevant to policy reform efforts. Analysts often speak of "needs assessment" and proceed to document the deficiencies that a policy change should address. "Assets analysis is the opposite of needs assessment. Where needs assessment determines deficiencies to be corrected, assets analysis identifies strengths to build on. . . . Those strengths or assets, if known, can be used to help clients meet their needs." If a diagnosis is based only on the needs in a community or an organization, designers may miss some of the most important characteristics of that community or organization. By consciously asking people to think of both needs and assets, groups can come to focus on a different set of characteristics.[26]

An example of the assets concept can be found in a growing number of studies of the strengths of community organizations in developing countries. Drawing from his experiences in Africa, Timberlake describes the explosion of community organizations in impoverished countries—groups that provide informal training, offer finances, and undertake irrigation and drainage activities, erosion control, and reforestation.[27] Nicholson expands on this point by noting that local "communities evince remarkable energy, ingenuity, and effectiveness in dealing with the collective challenges of development, when given an opportunity to do so."[28] The conceptual point is that by shifting from the concept of "need" to "assets," participants are stimulated to look for evidence of such contributions.

Systems Thinking. Systems thinking stimulates participants to focus on relationships and interdependencies. Individuals are asked to conceptualize a policy arena as a system of interdependent parts and to trace the interactions among these parts. Early uses of systems theory assumed "closed systems" in the sense that the elements and relations among them can be fully known and understood. Policy systems in LDCs are viewed as "open systems," indicating that the environment—political, economic, international—constantly influences the system. Openness also suggests that it is unlikely that one could identify all the relevant factors and that it is possible to omit important items or ignore incidental effects. A related concept is "soft systems"; it emphasizes the human factor in systems and the difficulty of identifying and measuring the relationships among the elements. Systems theory is very consistent with the nature of policy inquiry since it emphasizes the need to reconceptualize events and to appreciate the variety of influences on a problem and the myriad of results that can ensue from a changed policy. Its effect is to greatly expand the opportunities for introducing change into a policy area. A variety of techniques have been devised for diagramming or mapping systems—for example, tree diagrams and oval diagrams (see the following sections).[29] The challenge is to use them to reconceptualize problems but to avoid allowing the analysis to become overwhelmingly complex.

Matrix Thinking. A matrix crosses two dimensions, such as in a simple

2 x 2 set of cells. Whereas systems thinking helps people think about the complex relations among events, matrices can simplify and focus thinking. Matrices identify dimensions and then stimulate people to conceptualize about ways in which they interact in order to fill in the cells. The following example is based on Michael Patton's work. Assume a group is considering how to evaluate or monitor a series of activities. This matrix relates the nature of the activity to be monitored to the nature of the monitoring process.[30] It conceptualizes four kinds of monitoring and data collection procedures:

Nature of Monitoring Process	Nature of Activity Being Monitored	
	Routine	Nonroutine
Routine	A	C
Nonroutine	B	D

Cases in cell A can be handled with fairly routine data collection procedures since the goals and measures of the goals are clear. Cell B refers to cases where the goals are clear but the data about them will require some special treatment. For example, a policy to stimulate credit to poor farmers may have clear, identifiable goals, and hence is coded routine. However, the dynamics of making loans to poor farmers poses problems, and it would probably not be sufficient to simply compile data on the timeliness of repayments. Nonroutine procedures to interpret the findings would be necessary in order to fully understand farmer responses. In cell C the activity itself may be nonroutine, but once a monitoring system is set up, it could be continued in a fairly routinized manner. For example, some creative thinking would have to go into designing an effective way to monitor a nutrition education program. Once put in place, however, it could be carried out in a routine way. Cases that fall in cell D call for creative monitoring approaches to deal with unique situations. The use of a matrix helps participants conceptualize different tasks and explore how they compare and contrast with each other.

Patton suggests another example of a matrix based on the earlier distinction between assets and needs:

Assets	Needs	
	High	Low
High	A	C
Low	B	D

Matrices allow participants to conceptualize relationships first, and then apply the concepts to particular cases. In this example, participants could begin by speculating about the dynamics of providing services in each of these cells without reference to any particular community. For example, they would conceptualize the nature of service delivery in communities where both assets and needs were high and contrast this with service delivery where both were low. After working through the logic of each cell, they could determine where to locate the community of immediate interest to them, and use that as a takeoff point for projecting service delivery strategies.

Conceptualizing and matrix thinking not only stimulate new ways of thinking, they are also a valuable way to think systematically about qualitative data. It is common to assume that quantitative information can be handled with numbers and statistics whereas qualitative information has to be presented in narrative form. However, because of cognitive limitations, people can absorb only so much narrative description. Visual displays such as matrices and others presented in this section are techniques for organizing qualitative information in a more accessible manner to show patterns. But they are more than displays; they are also tools for analyzing situations.[31]

Structured Group Process Techniques

Avoiding Groupthink. Following on his analysis showing the prevalence of "groupthink," Janis proposes steps to avoid its limitations: Be aware that groupthink is possible, and try to consciously avoid it; look for biases in the preferred choice, particularly if there has been minimal disagreement and debate; divide into subgroups periodically and then reconvene and hammer out any differences; bring in outside experts to react to possible strategies; assign one member to be a devil's advocate and raise problems.[32]

Nominal Group Technique or Process. This technique, also known as NGT and the snowball technique, is the best-known version of a structured process. Participants follow a carefully prescribed series of steps: (1) individuals separately list alternative goals or solutions to a problem, (2) each alternative is presented in turn by group members until all ideas are presented, (3) alternatives may be clarified, but there cannot be any lobbying for or against, (4) members independently rank the alternatives, and (5) voting or mathematical pooling of individual rankings is used to establish group rankings and priorities.[33] By eliminating general discussion or lobbying for a view, NGT keeps individuals from manipulating group choices. The resulting choice reflects the underlying consensus or distribution of views within the group.

Consensus Mapping. This technique helps participants move beyond generating ideas and arrive at a consensus or priority ranking. Assume the group has generated ideas, clarified them and prioritized them, either through brainstorming or an NGT process. The next step is to map them and show their relations. To do this, members have to visualize relationships among the separate ideas, critically review them, and then organize them to produce a useful strategy. One technique uses a large wall and index cards or small sheets of paper which can be moved around on the wall. As the group discusses the multiple causes of a lack of credit, for example, each proposed cause can be written on a card and affixed to the wall in a place that shows its relationships to the other factors. Once the major elements are identified and located, participants look for clusters of ideas and try to agree as a group on how to classify them. Typically the group is faced with a complex array of ideas, which can be intimidating and confusing. According to this particular strategy, group leaders develop a "straw-man" map. It links the ideas in some fashion to provide a straw-man structure and give the group a specific proposal to react to and reorganize. Proponents claim that this tactic is more apt to produce a creative solution than alternatives such as allowing the group to brainstorm relations or select from a group of options.[34]

Conceptualizing System Relationships. One of the most effective strategies stimulates members to conceptualize a systemic view of a problem.[35] Called "mind mapping" in one study, it helps people let go of their old ideas and develop new concepts.[36] A problem is identified and members of a group are asked to brainstorm what factors contribute to it. As in NGT, there can be no debate about what to include. Oval diagramming is one version. Participants are asked to identify the different elements in a system and link them with connecting arrows. Members are given a problem, which is placed in an oval at the center of a sheet of paper posted for everyone to see. They are asked to think about the forces leading to the problem. Immediate causes are placed in smaller ovals surrounding it and more remote causes are placed at a greater distance. The nature of the relationship is identified with signs that indicate whether the relationship is positive or negative, direct or indirect. "The thought that goes into oval diagramming often uncovers relationships that may be the key to a further understanding of system behavior. Oval diagrams facilitate communication between analysts and decision makers by highlighting undesirable effects and relationships that require careful attention. By treating assumptions and hypotheses explicitly, oval diagrams may resolve discrepancies or deficiencies in the mental models used by decision makers."[37]

Stakeholder Analysis. "Stakeholder analysis" is useful when there are major conflicts within a group and when there is a need for new and innovative choices to be made. Participants begin by identifying all of the stake-holders—those who are either affected by or who affect the decision. This step forces the group to address the views of those who may otherwise be ignored or excluded. The group then looks at the preferred solutions of each stakeholder group and their assumptions in arriving at those solutions. Members may be asked to specifically present the case of some stakeholders if their concerns would not otherwise be included in the analysis. If the issue is how to improve the efficiency of agricultural marketing, the various stake-holders would be identified, their preferred solutions listed, and the assumptions implicit in each would be laid out. Group members would then try to pool the acceptable assumptions and craft a new way to think about the problem.[38]

PCL. In decisions that require a high level of acceptance, feelings among the participants are especially important. Problem-centered leadership (PCL) is a technique for enlisting group acceptance by dealing overtly with feelings from the outset. Leaders present problems in objective and unbiased ways and then stimulate broad participation and comment from the group. Essentially, PCL relies on leaders with effective group process skills in stimulating a discussion and promoting trust and effective interaction. Research comparing this approach with the more structured NGT process found that PCL produced less conflict in the group, led to greater group acceptance of the result, and provided decisions that were ranked higher on their technical quality.[39]

CONCLUSIONS

Since policy inquiry usually involves a sequence of decisions and events, different techniques may be used at different stages of the process. Most of the reports of process inquiry that will be referred to in Part Two draw from a number of these. The discussion here has linked the techniques to criteria for carrying out a policy inquiry and stressed their rationale so that those planning an inquiry process can select those most appropriate to the particular purposes of an event.

The framework described in Part Two builds on these same criteria (see Table 5.1). *Elicits alternative views:* It explores who should be included in the process to get a variety of perspectives (Chapter 6). *Generates new ideas:* It proposes techniques to generate new ideas in the course of diagnosing a situation (Chapter 7); it also separates issue definition from strategy planning in order to prevent people from avoiding issues that are difficult to deal with (Chapter 8). *Arrive at a choice:* The framework includes a step for designing specific strategies to cope with a problem (Chapter 9). *Deal with substance:* Throughout the several steps the framework points to substantive

Table 5.2. Group Process Techniques

Brainstorming. Generate alternative views in response to a question.

Conceptualizing. Abstract from reality to look at events in new ways.

Systems thinking. Identify components of some problem arena and speculate about relationships among them.

Matrix thinking. Identify dimensions of a problem or situation, usually two, and conceputalize how they interact.

Nominal group technique or process. Use a structured process with a group to generate alternative ideas and rank them.

Consensus mapping. Generate a synthesis among a number of alternatives.

Conceptualizing system relationships or mind mapping. Examine relationships among components of a system and with variables in the environment.

Stakeholder analysis. Identify and compare assumptions and views of competing stakeholders, including groups not present.

PCL, problem centered-leadership. Help a group deal openly with feelings in the process of reaching a decision.

issues that have proved critical in past experiences; it encourages participants to define particular substantive issues and to invite appropriate experts to participate. *Develop commitment:* The framework assumes that by involving people in the process they will have a greater commitment to the results, although as noted earlier the evidence for this is ambiguous. *Recognize feelings*: Experiences in conducting the sessions show that feelings can influence participation and responsiveness to change. Those applying the framework will need to deal with these in the course of analyzing problems and designing strategies.

NOTES

1. Janis, 1989, *Crucial Decisions,* 149ff.
2. Simon, 1985, "Human Nature," 295.
3. Christakis, 1985, "Systems Scientists," 21.
4. Kohli, 1989, "Economic Liberalization," 308.
5. Miner, 1979, "Comparative Analysis," 81; 1984, "Group Versus Individual."
6. Janis, 1989, *Crucial Deciscions.*
7. Angle, 1989, "Research," 164; Fiol and Lyles, 1985, "Organizational Learning."
8. Lindenberg, 1989, "Economic Adjustment."
9. Miner, 1979, "Comparative Analysis," 82.
10. Angle, 1989, "Research," 165.
11. Lovrich, 1989, "Simon/Argyris Debate," 470–474. See also Blunt, 1983, *Organizational Theory.*
12. Korten, 1984. "Strategic Organization," 341.

13. Eadie and Steinbacher, 1985, "Strategic Agenda Management," 424.

14. The International Development Management Center, University of Maryland, has been pursuing this approach in a number of consulting activities in LDCs. See Kettering, 1985, "Action Training"; Ingle, 1985, "Integrating Management"; Mickelwait, 1980, "Technical Assistance."

15. Silverman, et al., 1986, *Action-Planning Workshops*.

16. White, 1982, "Goal-Setting Process," 81.

17. Janis, 1972, *Groupthink*, 8; 1989, *Crucial Decisions*, 240.

18. Bryson, 1988, *Strategic Planning*.

19. Delbecq, et al., 1975, *Group Techniques*.

20. Delbecq, et al., 1975, *Group Techniques*, 16.

21. Mahler, 1987, "Structured Decision Making," 340, 341; Lindenberg and Crosby, 1981, *Managing Development*, 6f, also emphasize the value of political exchange.

22. Delp, et al., 1977, *Systems Tools*.

23. de Bono, 1970, *Lateral Thinking*, 149–165; Delp, 1977, *Systems Tools*, 3–5.

24. Delp, 1977, *Systems Tools*, 3.

25. Patton, 1981, *Creative Evaluation*, 76–79.

26. Patton, 1981, *Creative Evaluation*, 75–83.

27. Timberlake, 1985, *Africa*, 210–211. See also Korten, 1980, "Community Organization"; Uphoff, 1985, "Gal Oya"; Calavan, 1984, "Appropriate Administration."

28. Nicholson, 1989, "State of the Art," 23.

29. Delp, et al., 1977, *Systems Tools*, 67–106. The assumptions in a soft systems approach are described and applied to the LDC setting in Wilson and Morren, 1990, *Systems Approaches*.

30. Patton, 1981, *Creative Evaluation*. This discussion draws from his discussion of matrices, 123–144.

31. Miles and Huberman, 1984, *Qualitative Data*, 20–21.

32. Janis, 1989, *Crucial Decisions*, 209–224.

33. Mahler, 1987, "Structured Decision Making," 336.

34. Hart, et al., 1985, "Managing Complexity."

35. Churchman, 1968, *Systems Approach*, presents a good overview of systems theory.

36. Macadam, et al., 1989, "Strategic Planning," 5–6.

37. Delp, et al., 1977, *Systems Tools*, 80, 83.

38. Mitroff and Emshoff, 1979, "Strategic Assumption Making."

39. Miner, 1979, "Comparative Analysis."

PART TWO

A FRAMEWORK FOR A STRATEGIC PROCESS FOR POLICY CHANGE

6

Initiating and
Agreeing on a Process

CHARACTERISTICS OF THE PROCESS

Elements in the Framework

Part One presented a model of a policy inquiry process. Stated as a hypothesis, the model proposes that strategic inquiry will lead to more successful and sustained economic development than is the case when reforms are designed by fiat or when they neglect contending views and contextual conditions. There is evidence to support the hypothesis, but it is preliminary and is based largely on field evaluations by participants in strategic processes and on case studies of reforms. The evaluations consistently report that the process was a positive and informative experience. The majority of case studies, many noted throughout Part One, conclude that reforms need to be tailored to situations and that local officials should be involved more directly in designing them.

Part Two presents a framework drawn from the discussions in Part One. One dimension consists of steps in a strategic inquiry process—mapping the policy arena, defining major issues, and designing policies and implementation strategies. It emphasizes the direct involvement of relevant parties, the value of reconceptualizing situations, the importance of taking different views seriously, and the role that ideas and new information can play in stimulating change. It assumes change is possible if participants begin by assessing the characteristics of the environment and then look for strategic ways to intervene.

The second dimension consists of the five elements in policy reform packages as identified in Chapter 1: macro and sectoral policies; supporting sectoral investments; institutional analysis; human resource development; and mobilization of people, particularly the poor, to participate in economic growth. For each, participants analyze the nature of the problems they face, the political and social environment, and the capacity for implementing the changes (see Table 6.1).[1]

75

Table 6.1 A Framework for Designing and Implementing Policy Reforms

A Strategic Inquiry Process

ASPECTS OF SUCCESSFUL POLICY REFORMS	Diagnose Situation	Identify Major Issues	Develop Set of Coping Strategies
Macro and Sectoral Policies	Collaborative inquiry among several perspectives to gather OPINIONS and compile INFORMATION about three aspects of each element:		Strategies can include:
			Policy Changes and Adjustments
Supporting Sectoral Investments		**Participants**	Investment Decisions
Institutional Development		**Review** **Mapping and** **Agree on**	Institutional Designs
	NATURE OF PROBLEM		Strategies for Developing
Human Resource Development		**MAJOR**	Human Resources and Mobilizing Communities
	SOCIAL AND POLITICAL ENVIRONMENT	**ISSUES**	
Mobilization To Participate In Economic Development	IMPLEMENTA- TION CAPACITY		Political Strategies
			Implementation Plans

Chapter 7 describes how to reconceptualize problems by using analytic tools to map the situation, Chapter 8 deals with identifying issues, and Chapter 9 focuses on strategies. This chapter describes the general characteristics of the process and, in particular, examines how to plan and get it started. It draws on actual case studies to describe experiences in carrying out comparable events in LDCs.

Tensions in the Process

Several tensions are intrinsic to the process. First, one needs to strike a "balance between economically viable and politically feasible policies."[2] Economic crises in most LDCs are sufficiently severe that immediate and radical change is necessary. At the same time, past interventions underscore the folly of moving too fast, of ignoring social and political realities, and failing to appreciate the time it takes for new perceptions and institutions to evolve. There is a similar tension between coping with immediate problems and developing an institutional capacity. The problem is that immediate tasks easily consume available time and energy. Officials become frustrated and move ahead with the task even if means short-circuiting planning sessions and experiments; donor and government regulations press for accomplishing immediate benchmarks even if it means relying on expatriate initiatives.[3]

There are ways to resolve the tensions. Brinkerhoff and Ingle propose a "structured flexibility" approach that combines general guidelines and short-term tasks. "A plan is developed as a set of guideposts to deviate from as circumstances and accumulated knowledge dictate, instead of as a road map to be followed mechanically. . . . Structured flexibility fuses this long-term goal with short-term service/product delivery targets. That is, long-term capacity is created by generating products or services along the way."[4] Short-term activities not only accomplish tasks but also provide incentives to continue, and they encourage commitment to the longer-run activities. A recent study of technology transfer in LDCs similarly links "doing" and "learning." The usual model for learning new technologies is to first innovate, then invest, and then produce. The authors found, however, that LDCs do better when they reverse this process. LDC units can import a technology, use it and learn from it, and then invest and innovate. "Experience in production and investment is generally needed to know what is wanted and what is possible in the way of new products and processes. Acquiring this experience is not automatic, however. Nor is it rapid and effortless. It takes conscious effort over a long period of time."[5]

Variations in the Process

There are at least four scenarios for dealing with policy reforms, each of which includes different sets of actors:

1. High level officials and donors
2. Government officials and political groups
3. Implementing officials among different agencies
4. Agency officials and community groups

In addition to reflecting the interests of the players, scenarios vary according to the political context—how much conflict there is, how much information already exists, how much trust there is among the different stakeholders, and how much discretion there is for implementing units to explore options.

The process can also vary according to the sequence of events and the time frame. Variations include closely linked events occurring over a two-day period or a series of more loosely connected activities taking place throughout the year, with different participants in each. It could proceed in two phases. The first phase, in which participants focus on a very specific task such as developing a better information system so they gain confidence and experience, is followed by a second phase, in which they take a broader, more analytic view of what information is needed and how it will be used.

Interconnected Process

Another important characteristic is the interconnectedness of the process. The framework describes a series of steps for convenience, but in reality they are part of a single and iterative process. "Design and implementation are merged in that the project is modified and adapted as knowledge is acquired about the specific environment."[6] Policies can be reviewed and altered throughout the implementation process. Even where there is agreement on a broad policy goal such as improving agricultural productivity, the details are usually not fixed. Initial plans can be reviewed and changed; goals can be redefined; additional participants can be included at various stages; and new information can be sought.

DECIDING WHO SHOULD BE INVOLVED

Selecting participats is critically important since the outcome of any process is shaped by those who take part in it. From a pragmatic perspective, there are two criteria for selecting participants: both the practical—what key operational personnel should be here?—and the political—who must be invited because their cooperation is needed?"[7] The point is to bring together those responsible for designing policies, those involved in implementing them, and any others who have a stake in the policies. The list may include potential opponents. "The wise change agent will discover where those pockets of resistance lie and move to anticipate them before they develop and coalesce into strong opposition. The principle of including in the decision-making those who have something to lose is one proven method of meeting the needs of the potential loser. The outcome can often be a creative solution or a workable compromise."[8]

The framework suggests one other criterion—select participants partly with an eye to the quality and dynamics of policy inquiry itself. One purpose of the process is to help people break out of a business-as-usual frame of mind, look at issues in new ways and explore new roles. This criterion suggests selecting some to present different perspectives and options. There is some circularity at work here. Selecting participants depends on how the policy problem is defined, but how the situation is defined depends on who is initially involved. This criterion simply adds that the quality of the debate be considered in selecting participants.

Participants vary according to the four scenarios noted earlier. In one scenario, high-level officials and donor representatives come together, usually to discuss a general outline for policy changes. Chapter 4 described these as occasions for raising political issues and for including political officials and representatives as well as technocratic staff. A major purpose in this scenario is to increase the sensitivity of donors to the political costs of proposed changes.[9]

A second scenario involves government policymakers and representatives of other institutions in the society—church, union, and business leaders, for example. In reality, planning is often done by technocratic staff and top political officials. Kaufman describes how policy reforms in Brazil and Argentina during the 1980s were designed in highly secretive sessions among government economists and top leaders. The proposals, couched in economic arguments, were clearly designed around the political interests of the leaders, but there was no consultation with political groups.[10] Although there are times when it may be wise to insulate the leadership, a number of cases indicate otherwise. Joan Nelson, for example, concludes that "frank and vigorous campaigns of explanation and persuasion can be quite effective in winning temporary public acquiescence, and gaining union acceptance of wage restraint."

It is important to appreciate that groups are usually being asked to make different kinds of sacrifice and these costs will undoubtedly influence their conduct during the session. For example, the public and unions are typically asked to tighten their belts, whereas businesspeople, "investors and entrepreneurs are asked to consider new options, take new risks, write off (at least in part) old investments, and generally change their ways of doing business." As a result, the latter may be less amenable to persuasion, and require different kinds of incentives.[12] Irving Horowitz, on the other hand, argues that reforms usually require more sacrifice by the poor, and warns that discussions among political interests can obscure the different levels of sacrifice. Typically, those promoting liberalizing reforms ask the wealthy to be a little more politically conscious of competing interests. At the same time they ask the poor to be "less concerned with their private needs and more concerned with their political responsibilities."[13] The different appeals may unleash resentment.

A third scenario includes primarily implementing officials, drawn from one or several agencies. Here the problems are more apt to deal with agency lines of accountability and the need for cooperation or coordination among units. The group should have close ties with policy-level officials, either by including them in the discussions or reporting to them, in order to link policy definition and implementation plans. The need for "time and place information" means that these discussions should include implementing staff—both midlevel managers and field staff. Their inclusion is based on several assumptions. First, those involved are more likely to be committed to the strategies and energetic in carrying them out. Second, people throughout an organization are important sources of information and feedback, both to map the current situation and design an alternative strategy. Third, operational staff are often the source of innovation. As Robert Reich puts it, "Because production is a continuous process of reinvention, entrepreneurial efforts must be focused on many thousands of small ideas rather than a few big ones. . . . Workers . . . are cultivated as fonts of valuable up-to-the-minute information about how things can be improved. Because the information and expertise are dispersed throughout the organization, top management does not solve problems nor set specific direction; it creates an environment in which people can identify and solve problems for themselves."[14]

A fourth scenario includes agency managers and representatives from community groups or beneficiaries. Like officials located at different levels in the organization, they have particular knowledge about existing practices and possible alternatives. Beneficiaries may be able to break through the insular, bureaucratic outlook of staff, and may also encourage local communities to assume some responsibility for activities.

Whichever scenario or combination, studies show there is little chance of success unless top-level officials are supportive and involved at some point in a strategic planning process. Depending on the policy in question, top officials may include both politicians and administrators. Even if they are not directly involved, they need to give their blessing to the process and hopefully contribute some time and resources. Studies indicate that top officials are most apt to become involved if they have a felt need for change and perceive a problem that needs to be addressed.[15]

There is some disagreement about the value of diversity. A review of planning workshops by World Bank staff cautions against too much diversity. The reviewers found that workshops were most productive when those involved in the initial stages were close in status. Top-level managers can inhibit representatives of citizen groups or lower-level staff. In later stages of the process diversity is less of a problem.[16] However, according to the third criterion stated earlier—ensuring the quality of the inquiry process—diversity can be useful. If one purpose is to get those at top levels to listen to different perspectives, community members and operating staff can play an important role.[17] The structured techniques described in Chapter 5 may be the best way to manage diversity.

Different groups can also be involved at various stages. A strategic approach to improving irrigation practices in Pakistan used a series of workshops in different provinces. The first involved thirty to thirty-five people from twelve or thirteen organizations, including both field and operational management levels from all of the implementing units. A second workshop brought together people from all of the implementing units, but relied on a smaller group to plan the operations. The plans devised by this group were then circulated among executives and policy-level personnel for their approval during yet a third phase.[18]

GETTING STARTED

If strategic thinking is a new experience, participants need to be introduced to its purpose and convinced of its utility. As noted earlier, strategic analysis is often more difficult to apply in the public sector than in the private sector. Organizations are often larger, lack the accountability of markets, and are subject to more external pressures. It is even more difficult to apply in the Third World, where organizations tend to be rule-bound, and where managers focus on narrow, operational routines and are less apt to think strategically.

Participants need to perceive that a strategic approach can help them address their immediate situation. Sometimes it will be helpful to think in terms of solving a specific problem; sometimes it is more appropriate to think in terms of learning to cope with situations. According to one review of strategic approaches, the important purpose is helping people "gain the skills to remove or work through the constraints in the system. Often the issue is not that the client does not know what is right (or even how to do it right) but that he/she is constrained or prevented from doing it."[19] Getting started usually involves the following:

- Identify the policy relevant problems
- Introduce the concept of strategic analysis
- Explore its relevance to the situation
- Agree that the process is worthwhile

Because participants may need to experience strategic analysis before they can appreciate its purpose, an initial workshop to introduce the process may be necessary. For example, a group assisting local governments with their water and sanitation facilities wanted officials to do a strategic analysis of their capacity for designing an effective system. They found that participants first had to experience what such an analysis would entail. Consultants began by interviewing staff at all levels to ask what problems they were experiencing. "These data were then analyzed for patterns, and consensus and workshop goals were developed. Top- and middle-level managers were then brought together and the data were revealed. Small problem-solving groups then worked on solutions and made recommendations. Follow-up responsibilities were assigned to task forces and individuals, and a monitoring procedure was defined."[20]

A neutral third party may initiate the process. A series of dialogue seminars conducted by INCAE, a management training institute in the Caribbean, illustrates this strategy. In separate efforts in countries throughout the region (thirty-six events in 1988 alone), the institute brought together leaders from the public and private sectors, including church, labor, and military groups.

Institute faculty led guided discussions to help participants identify their critical problems, build consensus, and come to some initial agreement about possible strategies. Marc Lindenberg, a major architect of the sessions, drew several lessons: it was important to establish clear rules about the conduct of the sessions; participatory techniques were helpful in building consensus; presentation of comparable policy reform experiences proved instructive; follow-up workshops to study specific problems were helpful; and the seminars developed leadership within the political parties and private sector groups.[21]

The government can also establish a special unit to be in charge of analysis, with a mandate to bring different units together and sponsor workshops and seminars on policy issues. Such a committee established in the Dominican Republic to review and develop agricultural policy was composed of people from both the public and private sectors. They, in turn, set up an Agricultural Studies Unit (UEA), a small group of specialists to arrange for studies and contract with private firms to promote strategic planning sessions. "An innovative process introduced by the coordinator, which was not contemplated in the project paper, was to conduct brainstorming sessions involving key local policy makers and experts." Evaluations of the process underscored its evolving nature and the importance of assigning responsibility for strategic analysis to a free-standing unit that could bring other units together. At the same time, the unit remained small enough that it did not threaten the existing analytic units within the various ministries.[22]

Someone has to initiate the process, usually high-level or key officials who may sponsor the process themselves or assign it to others. Typically consultants are asked to set the process in motion. In most cases they begin by collecting data. Officials and staff are asked through interviews or during workshops to reflect on their situations and identify their problems. Officials are then brought together in a workshop setting and the results are fed back to them for reflection. A variation relies on a "learn by doing" approach, in which strategic management concepts are introduced to staff while they carry out a specific task. They learn about the approach while doing it. One group used a regular evaluation as an opportunity to introduce a strategic planning process. In the course of designing the evaluation, staff practiced a strategic analysis and then the evaluation team helped them set up a unit to be responsible for strategic planning in the future.[23]

A report of a strategic planning activity in Pakistan to improve the management of irrigated agriculture described the planning period as follows (adapted from original): "The entry phase varied from between one-and-a-half weeks to four days. During this period we attempted to meet with all the key actors in the province, as well as the project manager and his staff, to get their input, involvement, and support for the program; to identify who needed to be involved; to review the results of an earlier diagnostic study; to identify the concerns and issues that needed to be addressed. Typically we met with the Secretaries of Irrigation and Agriculture, the Chief Engineers, the Directors-General and the Directors beneath them, the operational counterparts of the project manager in each line agency, and other key players at the operational and policy levels."[24]

A report on a workshop to introduce strategic management concepts into the Ministry of Agriculture in Guinea noted the following steps. A team of expatriates began by informally talking with key individuals about their situation. They then held a workshop for senior officials, including department heads, chief financial officers of each department, and their respective assistants—fifteen people in all. They asked these officials to meet in small groups and reflect on the general purposes of a budget and report their conclusions to the larger group. In the next step, the officials had to apply these conclusions about the purpose of a budget to a specific line-item budget. They reflected on how well this budget fulfilled the purposes they had earlier laid out. Finally, the leaders introduced an alternative budget approach that encouraged strategic analysis by using programmatic categories rather than line items.[25]

In yet another example, a workshop was designed to introduce strategic management concepts to a group of officials from several countries. Participants were given two cases about specific economic problems to read and later discuss in the group. Strategic analysis was then introduced as a way to think about the two cases. Participants were next given readings on the public corporate sector and the economic crisis in the Philippines. Finally, they participated in a simulation in which they designed a strategic approach to reform the Filipino corporate sector.[26]

A similar workshop was held in the Philippines to introduce strategic thinking about higher education in agriculture to educators, in light of a government proposal to rationalize the higher education system. University officials throughout the country attended. In the opening session three experts introduced strategic thinking about agriculture. They emphasized the need to think about the rapidly changing environment and to think of agriculture as a total system rather than to focus on a single crop or technology. In the afternoon participants broke into small groups to apply the concepts to their situations. The report of the session noted that initially there was a lot of discomfort about participating in small groups and that leaders had to reassure participants that the format was really open-ended.[27]

AGREEING ON AN INITIAL DESIGN FOR THE PROCESS

Strategic management exercises can vary from a fairly short and structured event in which participants focus on a few specific aspects of a policy change to a more comprehensive and longer-range set of activities to redesign economic policies or institutions. Since strategic means selecting critical problems where change is feasible, those planning such an approach need to be strategic in deciding how to structure the process. They can review the process steps and substantive issues listed in Table 6.1 and agree on which parts are most relevant to their problems and situation. They also need to consider the time frame and participants. Scenarios one and two—those discussing broad policy agendas—are probably best handled through short workshops that enable officials to consider policy options; scenarios three and four—those involved more directly with implementation—are more apt to require a series of workshops over a longer time period that enable officials to experiment and make adjustments.

If participants are experiencing this approach for the first time, it may be wise to embark on a relatively limited effort, to introduce the approach and give participants an initial positive experience. Strategic planning can be very costly in terms of time and interpersonal activities, and reducing complexity may be valuable. At the same time, changes in thinking take time and little may happen if the process is too restricted. Those involved in planning need to also consider what technical expertise is needed, both for substantive issues and management strategies such as financial management and information systems. Since relevant expertise may become evident only at later stages in the process, planning will be ongoing and consultants can be brought in as the need arises.

MANAGING THE DYNAMICS OF THE PROCESS

The open-ended and participatory norms of a strategic process workshop can be unsettling and even threatening. Such disquiet is common in most settings, but is particularly prevalent in LDCs. A recent study of innovation in developing societies suggests concepts that can help observers anticipate when change will be particularly disconcerting. The study described peoples' values on four dimensions: hierarchy or collegiality, certainty or risk taking, a collectivist or individualistic orientation, and an achievement or service orientation. Those who ascribe to the first value on each dimension—hierarchy, certainty, collectivism, achievement—are more apt to resist and be uncomfortable with change and participatory planning. When participants share these values, it becomes necessary to "provide sufficient resources to reorient and retrain managers and staff in the values that the new management strategies require."[28]

Initial reluctance and even resistance can be a normal part of workshop experiences, which tend to go through four stages: (1) *forming*—participants come together and get to know each other; (2) *storming*—individuals resist the sessions and try to test the group norms; (3) *norming*—participants develop a group spirit and begin to feel more positive about the workshop; and (4) *performing*—participants become engaged in the task. The point of conceptualizing such a sequence is to show that it is normal to move from being tentative and reserved, and even resentful, to being more actively involved.[29]

These dynamics are illustrated in a workshop held to design a training program. Participants were African government officials, trainers, and a few donor agency staff, mostly women. Their task was to design a program for African institutes that would address the needs of women. The first step was to engage participants in making a strategic analysis of their task. A planning group met ahead of time and proposed that in order to train women, they would first have to help women see the choices available to them and identify their needs. The planning group prepared a four-page think piece to introduce their conceptual definition of the task and disseminated it to participants ahead of time. In the initial meeting, participants were asked to discuss this formulation and decide if a focus on management training for women's organizations was the appropriate way to define the issue.

Participants had a hard time focusing on the question, however. They did not know each other and had not built up sufficient understanding of each other's agendas to feel comfortable contributing to the discussion. On the second day, facilitators succeeded in bringing some focus to the discussion by recording points on flip charts, but there was still a lack of focus. Toward the end of that day, one person said, "Let's talk about what women do, and not about problems of organizations." As soon as the participants moved from an abstraction, such as management problems in organizations, to specifics, the discussion took off. Later they were able to return to the original proposition and focus at a more analytic level on problems and needs. Similarly, when the leaders presented an agenda on the first day, participants were unable to respond to it right away. They had to experience it first, reflect on it, and then modify it as they went along.[30] By the afternoon of the second day, the participants understood better what the donors proposing the project hoped to get from the meeting. They also had developed a sense of trust in others, and a confidence that they could make a contribution. As a result the discussion was both more focused and more dynamic.

CONCLUSIONS

The form of strategic policy inquiry varies according to the purposes of the sessions, the agendas of those sponsoring them and the likely participants. The framework (see Table 6.1) proposes a series of activities that engage participants in diagnosing their situations, defining major issues, and developing strategies to deal with the issues. Participants can use the framework to identify what should be covered. They need to consider which of the several aspects of policy reforms identified in the framework they should focus on, what sequence of planning activities is feasible, and who should be included in and responsible for different phases of the discussions. They also need to identify some group or unit to be responsible for overseeing the process.

Careful thought needs to go into introducing strategic thinking and such techniques as conceptualizing and brainstorming. Otherwise, groups may fall into old patterns of deferring to top-down mandates and adopting seemingly obvious and routine decisions. Designers should view the sessions as a way to introduce new ways of thinking and to think strategically about policies and implementation strategies. They also need to think strategically about the workshop sessions and appreciate that participants may feel threatened by some of the techniques.

NOTES

1. A review of USAID efforts to assist with policy reforms noted this emphasis and agreed that more attention needed to be paid to studying results of reforms and improving capacity. Compare similar frameworks. Lindenberg and Crosby, 1981, *Managing Development,* propose a framework that emphasizes political strategies. Lindenberg, 1989, "Economic Adjustment," 362, proposes dealing with four questions in these sessions: What is the purpose of a proposed policy? Who will benefit and lose? How have others handled similar changes? What strategy could be used here? Brinkerhoff, 1990, *Program Performance,* presents a framework that stresses the influences on performance.

2. Lindenberg, 1989, "Economic Adjustment," 359; Callaghy, 1989, "State Capability"; J. Nelson, 1989, "Long-Haul Economic Reform"; and Grindle and Thomas, 1989, "Policy Makers," also stress this point.

3. Brinkerhoff and Ingle, 1989, "Structured Flexibility," stress the importance of donor regulations.

4. Brinkerhoff and Ingle, 1989, "Structured Flexibility," 490–491. See also Brinkerhoff, 1990, *Improving Development.*

5. Dahlman, et al., 1987, "Technological Development," 764.

6. Kahler, 1989, "International Financial Institutions," 151.

7. Silverman, et al., 1986, *Action-Planning Workshops,* 23. See also Lindenberg and Crosby, 1981, *Managing Development,* 38.

8. Edwards, 1988, *Managing Institutional Development,* 24.

9. Kahler, 1989, "International Financial Institutions," 151; Kaufman, 1989, "Politics."

10. Kaufman, 19189, "Politics."

11. J. Nelson, 1984, "Political Economy," 998. See also comments by Lindenberg, 1989, "Economic Adjustment," and Kaufman, 1989, "Politics."

12. J. Nelson, 1984, "Political Economy," 998.

13. I. Horowitz, 1987, "Roshomon Effect," 106.

14. Reich, 1983, *American Frontier,* 123.

15. Hage and Finsterbusch, 1987, *Organizational Change.*

16. Silverman, et al., 1986, *Action-Planning Workshops*, 23–24.

17. Korten, 1980, "Community Organization."

18. Jones and Clyma, 1986, "Management Improvement," 29–30. This work was sponsored by Colorado State University and the University of Maryland, and is part of the Performance Management Project, funded by USAID.

19. Edwards, 1988, *Managing Institutional Development*, 17.

20. Edwards, 1988, *Managing Institutional Development*, 8.

21. Marc Lindenberg, presentation at workshop on policy reforms, Agency for International Development, May 1989.

22. Church and Castro, 1988, *Agricultural Policy*, 4–10.

23. Macadam, et al., 1989, *Strategic Planning*, iii.

24. Jones and Clyma, 1986, "Management Improvement," 24.

25. Report on Introductory Workshop on Program and Budget Planning, Ministry of Agriculture and Animal Resources, Conakry, Republic of Guinea, May 26, 1989.

26. World Bank Workshop on Strategic Management, May 16, 1985.

27. Report of the Seminar on Strategic Planning for Tertiary Agricultural Education, August 12, 1988, Manila. This and similar experiences are elaborated in Wilson and Morren, 1990, *Systems Approaches*.

28. Rondinelli, et al., 1986, "Contingency Planning," 51.

29. Silverman, et al., 1986, *Action-Planning Workshops*, 10–11.

30. Elisabeth Shields, Economic Development Institute, World Bank, Field Notes for Workshop on Role of Regional Training Institutes, Douala, Cameroon, December 1989.

7

Diagnosing the Policy Arena

CHARACTERISTICS OF MAPPING

The inquiry process described here follows three steps: diagnosing the situation, identifying issues, and developing strategies. While it is possible, and often desirable, to adapt this sequence to specific cases, it is important to keep these steps separate. Typically participants identify an immediate problem and decide what to do about it. If the problem lies in rapid turnover of personnel, for example, the obvious strategy is to hire more personnel. Policy inquiry and strategic analysis, however, assume that participants need to look at their situation from new and alternative perspectives. They need to examine why there is a rapid turnover, consider if there are alternative ways of getting a job done, and review their personnel practices. Based on this diagnosis or mapping exercise, the subject of Chapter 7, they need to identify the nature of the problem they face, the subject of Chapter 8. Only when they have conceptually worked their way through these two steps do they move on to develop strategies, the subject of Chapter 9. Collapsing the process makes it harder to see the underlying dynamics or propose innovations.

The framework in Table 6.1 can be used to make the diagnosis more systematic. It lists the five aspects of sustainable policy reforms that were described in Chapter 1. For each of these, the framework specifies that participants should map the nature of the problem, the social and political environment, and the capacity for implementing the strategies. A caveat that Lindenberg and Crosby attach to their work is also appropriate here. "The important feature of the overall approach is not the use of checklists . . . but the ability to think logically about political problems in the future. The checklists and frameworks can serve as learning devices, but are not meant as a substitute for analytic thinking.[1]

First, some general comments about mapping.

Mapping Through Opinions and Descriptive Information

There are two kinds of information for diagnosing a situation. One consists of *perceptions and opinions* about a situation. Participants typically have diverse perspectives on events and hold to different causal models about which policies and activities will generate greater productivity. One purpose of mapping is to document this variety and determine areas of agreement and disagreement. Do the disagreements stem from a lack of information or from different values and interests? The second kind of information is *descriptive data*. Conceptualizing exercises identify needed information and those responsible for gathering it.

Organizations can constrain opinions by socializing members into looking at problems through the prism of organizational norms. Techniques need to break through these confining norms and encourage members to look at events from alternative perspectives. Brainstorming sessions and structured techniques for gathering information, described in Chapter 5, can generate a variety of perceptions, ensure that a few do not dominate the sessions, and encourage minority views. If some relevant interests are not part of the workshop group, then techniques such as an assigned "devil's advocate" may be employed.[2]

Data collection techniques about the setting are similarly varied. In general, participants should be strategic in defining what information they need, and avoid the common tendency to collect reams of data for their own sake.[3] They should consider "rapid reconnaissance" strategies that use proxy measures and readily available evidence as alternatives to rigorous surveys and sampling techniques.[4] At the same time, as Honadle reminds us, there are dangers. Since one of the goals of strategic analysis is to break out of traditional ways of thinking, the lack of rigor allows participants to collect information, perhaps unwittingly, that reinforces their preconceptions.[5]

Conceptualizing Problems and Opportunities

Strategic analysis attempts to conceptualize tasks and settings in new ways so that participants can find ways to introduce change into their situation. Participants need to balance descriptions of what exists with concepts that lead them to think about their setting from a fresh angle and anticipate problems that may arise. One conceptual technique is called SWOT analysis, an acronym that refers to Strengths, Weaknesses, Opportunities, and Threats.[6] Participants identify the opportunities and threats in the setting, and note the strengths and weaknesses in proposed policies and strategies. Later in the process these same items can be used to develop a strategy for implementing the policy changes.[7] A matrix could also be developed in which one dimension lays out the elements in a policy, while the other consists of the SWOTs. For each element or objective, participants would consider the strengths, weaknesses, opportunities, and threats.[8] SWOTS, like assets analysis mentioned in Chapter 5, are designed to stimulate participants to focus on both problems and supports.

An analysis of issues that can arise in developing a policy to promote the private sector illustrates the uses of SWOT. The diagnosis may indicate that there are no banking or credit facilities in rural areas, clearly a weakness. At the same time it might find that local community organizations have formed savings groups, a strength, and that there are a number of active voluntary groups in the region, an opportunity. The analysis might also suggest that if private credit institutions were established, they would be reluctant to provide loans to the poorer farmers, possibly a threat. After mapping these, participants would design an appropriate strategy. It might provide seed capital to the nonprofits to develop a revolving credit program and assist the community in monitoring the loans and repayments. Or it could expand private sector banking and include regulations to ensure that poorer farmers could qualify for the loans.[9]

Multiple Perspectives

There is a growing appreciation that social and political tensions, culture, and institutions all have an effect on economic productivity. This multiplicity of influences poses two problems for mapping exercises. First, policy reforms and implementation plans typically focus on economic and financial aspects of the environment and exclude other factors. By defining the arena of influence narrowly, some opportunities and threats are overlooked.[10] Qualitative aspects of a situation, such as the "norms of the organization," or the "cultural context" may be ignored because their effects are often subtle and it is hard to collect clear information about them. Nevertheless, they may offer the greatest threats to designing and implementing effective reforms.

The second problem is that groups can be intimidated by having to consider multiple factors, and some balance between being inclusive and being selective is helpful. One strategy distinguishes among those parts of the environment that officials have to simply take into account or acknowledge, parts over which they are likely to have some influence, and parts where they exercise control.[11] Normally environmental mapping focuses on aspects where officials are likely to have an influence, but even this can be ambiguous. Another way to manage the complexity is to carry out mapping in stages. It is not necessary to exhaustively map a situation before going on to identify issues and design strategies. A preliminary mapping session may be sufficient to develop an initial pilot strategy to implement part of a policy and produce further information about the situation.[12] As one gets into the mapping exercise, new questions will arise and lead to follow-up data gathering.

Conceptual analyses can be frustrating if they become too abstract or are too open-ended. For example, a SWOT analysis was used by a group analyzing the environment of an agricultural research project. After spending a day working with the SWOT categories, the group became frustrated about spending so much time on discussions they felt were preliminary to the main event—identifying their specific tasks. The planning team, however, wanted the group to think about the situation from multiple perspectives. Strategically they decided to move on to examine a specific task and later returned to more conceptual discussions as opportunities arose.[13]

Another way to provide some structure to the mapping process is to carry out a historical analysis of a policy problem. It can be an open-ended case history, or the study could focus on a significant issue. For example, a group examining how to expand the private sector could brainstorm about the constraints on the private sector and decide to focus on the legal and regulatory environment. They could then carry out a historical analysis of the incentives and disincentives in present laws and regulations and compare the impact of alternative regulations.

The rest of this chapter returns to the aspects of policy reforms identified in the framework—macro and sectoral economic reforms, supporting sectoral investments, institutional development, human resource development, and mobilization. According to the framework, each is mapped according to the nature of the major problems that have arisen, the characteristics of the social and political environment, and the capacity for implementing proposed changes. The discussion suggests a number of concepts that could be used in mapping based on the earlier review of policy reforms. They are illustrative only since the most useful concepts and matrices will be developed by those immersed in analyzing a particular policy change for a particular situation. Nevertheless, they emphasize that mapping sessions have to go beyond exploring group sentiments and need to deal with substantive issues.

MAPPING MACRO AND SECTORAL LEVEL ECONOMIC POLICY ARENAS

The Nature of Macro and Sectoral Economic Problems

Perspectives on the causes of economic difficulties inevitably reflect different opinions and values. People differ, for example, about the relative importance of internal and external causes of economic problems and whether they are extrapolating from past experience or speculating about the future. The following matrix invites mapping on these dimensions.

Time Frame	Influences on Economic Development	
	External factors	Internal factors
Historical Record		
Current Activities		
Future Trends		

Including the historical record can make a difference, a point illustrated by discussions about the private sector. According to Bienen and Waterbury, public sector enterprises were originally expanded for a number of reasons —to meet equity goals, to compensate for weaknesses in the private sector, to limit the role of foreigners in the economy, to build national strength, and so forth. A counterargument states that privatization is currently being pursued because of the failure of the public sector, and that these historical and more ideological arguments carry little weight at the present time. Bienen and Waterbury, however, find that the historical arguments may still have an influence and that strategies to increase the role of the private sector will be more successful if they take these arguments into account. "Privatizations that strengthen the indigenous private sector will be more feasible than those that cast aside old concerns for economic sovereignty by selling important assets (steel mills, mines, the national airline) to foreign buyers. . . . It may be possible for new regimes or new political coalitions to break with past policies and obligations, but the origins and ideological rationales for state interventionism do play a role in shaping the course of privatization."[14]

There is also merit in mapping external forces in addition to the usual emphasis by international institutions on internal characteristics.[15] Mapping external factors could point to the fall in commodity prices for LDC exports (1989 average commodity prices were 35 percent below their level in 1980), the decline in the world aggregate demand for LDC exports, the worsening terms of trade, and the increase in real interest rates—trends that are likely to increase during the 1990s.[16] Including them allows country officials to explore ways to cope with the trends and sensitize donor officials to the extent of the problem these countries face.[17]

Experiences with reforms in Argentina, Brazil, and Mexico illustrate this interdependence of internal and external factors. Heavy indebtedness has forced these countries to make large interest payments and has led creditors to cut off access to private credit markets. The creditor governments, banks, and international lenders, in the meantime, have focused on problems internal to the countries and insisted that debt problems be handled on a case-by-case basis. This argument has deprived "debtors of significant leverage over creditor-country trade, monetary and fiscal policies that vitally affected their capacity to pay."[18] Kaufman continues that internal political pressures have encouraged LDC officials to accept this emphasis on internal adjustment efforts. Business interests do not want to oppose creditors because the latter could reduce short-term trade credit or disrupt vital imports. In addition, business interests worry that confrontations with external powers could be translated into populist appeals within the country that would threaten their interests. The result is a classic prisoners' dilemma situation. Each LDC pursues a rational strategy, but the net effect is a pattern of bargaining that is "heavily weighted toward creditor interests." Various plans have been discussed among international actors to reduce the debt. "As in the past, however, debtor countries played no more than a marginal role in the formulation of such plans; and until they can, it is unclear whether even the most powerful of these countries will be able to avoid absorbing the major costs of adjustment themselves."[19]

The matrix presented earlier could be made more specific by focusing on a particular problem and analyzing the external and internal factors contributing to it. Mittleman, for example, argues that the key problem in pursuing economic development is to generate savings to increase capital accumulation for investing in future development.[20] LDCs, he argues, need to garner resources both externally and internally if they are to avoid being vulnerable to the international economy. Brazil's strategy of embracing global capitalism and China's strategy of "going it alone" have both failed. His analysis suggests the following matrix:

	Resources for Economic Investments	
Time Frame	External Sources	Internal Sources
Historical Record		
Present Investment		
Future Trends		

Mapping the Political and Social Environment

Aspects of the social and political environment to be mapped include behavior patterns in a society, winners and losers from present practices, and projected changes and attitudes to growth among the populace.

Policies as Incentive Structures. Since actions to liberalize policies assume that price incentives will change behavior, social mapping is needed to determine the accuracy of this assumption. First, it is important to know who will be affected by proposed changes. A study of grain-producing areas in five African countries found that only 50 percent or less of rural agricultural households that carried out food crop agriculture were net sellers of major staples. This finding meant that policies to raise the prices of food staples would actually reduce the incomes of large numbers in rural areas.[21] Second, it is important to know about behavior patterns of affected groups. Recall the study of small farmer behavior in Senegal described in Chapter 2 that demonstrated the relevance of cultural practices to economic decisions. To anticipate how price changes will affect farmers' wages, job intentions, purchasing power, and productivity, information could be collected on the following: reasons for low productivity; access to additional land and inputs; how people derive and spend their income; how price changes affect consumption; and access to goods on which to spend additional income.

Assessing Winners and Losers. In general, publics have opposed austerity measures and encouraged expansionary government policies. Studies of the effects of elections on economic policies in Latin America, for example, document that electoral pressures have made it very difficult for governments to reduce fiscal deficits.[22] Mapping can approach this problem by dealing with three issues. First, based on an economic calculus, who are the likely beneficiaries and losers from a particular policy? Economic analyses can anticipate the objective impacts of policies, usually by examining estimated costs and benefits. Second, what are the subjective perceptions of the impacts as seen by the affected groups? Peoples' subjective estimates can vary from economic estimates. "In Malaysia in 1976, lower income Malays perceived that government rural development programs had improved their income levels and well being. Their support for the government increased even though more careful economic analysis by the World Bank showed no gains in real family income. In other cases, though it can be demonstrated that members of one group have made important gains, they may still be highly discontented if they believe that they did not gain as much as they should have."[23]

A third question concerns the organization and political visibility of the different groups. It is a well-known maxim of the politics of policy reform that raising producer prices and reducing public expenditures on subsidies and public services benefits rural interests and imposes major costs on urban interests, including the poor. Since urban groups are better organized and more visible, leaders generally defer to them. Leaders still have some leeway, however. Joan Nelson studied thirteen instances in which prices on food staples were raised, and found that there were riots in only three of the cases.[24]

General Sentiments About Growth as a National Strategy. Some countries, particularly where the economy has gone through a severe crisis, or where there has been strong leadership, have forged a national commitment to economic growth, and the leaders have been able to take strong actions to alter economic institutions. Korea and Indonesia are examples.[25] Mapping could examine the conditions for developing a commitment and look at such factors as public awareness of economic crisis, existence of accurate and understandable economic analyses of the present crisis, and available leadership to promote such support.

Mapping Capacity for Implementing the Reforms

Implementation problems are receiving increased attention, although, according to a World Bank study, delays in implementation are inevitable. "They reflect the unpredictability of the political difficulties governments face in implementing reforms rather than necessarily as a sign of poor design or dialogue."[26] The following five issues related to macro and sectoral policies have proved to affect implementation.

Core Economic Instruments For Managing the Economy. Mapping should examine the capacity of central ministries of finance and treasury and of central banks to control indebtedness and to use the budget to control expenditures. Does the Central Bank or Treasury control the authority to incur debt, and are they able to monitor and reform debt planning? Does the Finance Ministry have the power to review and manage policies, to plan, and to appraise public investments? How are budgets prepared and managed?

Data Collection and Analysis Capacity. The capacity to simply collect and evaluate information about expenditures and revenues is often severely inadequate. A study of reforms in Brazil, Argentina, and Mexico concluded that even in these countries, with their relatively sophisticated bureaucracies, there was, for example, "no fully reliable information about the number of enterprises in the state sector, since some enterprises existed only on paper; and others held more than one charter."[27] (Lack of analytic capacity is not necessarily an oversight, however, since political officials may be wary of skilled technocrats.[28]) A strategic analysis of agricultural policymaking in the Dominican Republic also concluded that the capacity for analysis was critical. Participants mapped the following constraints on good analysis: policymaking was influenced by partisan politics, and analytic evidence had very little influence; the agricultural sector had a severe shortage of trained technical staff; national economic policies received little analysis before being enacted; the multiplicity of public sector institutions added confusion; implementation was fragmented among the institutions; there was no ongoing monitoring or evaluation of policies; and there were no mechanisms for involving private firms in doing analysis.[29]

Linkages Among Policy Incentives. Policies are often linked to others in such a way that they have to be carefully sequenced or timed, adding to normal implementation difficulties. For example, a privatization program may include dismantling of a parastatal, training in small enterprise management, small business loans to potential entrepreneurs, and trade liberalization in processing firms. Mapping needs to examine what actions a proposed policy change is related to or dependent on. Is the policy part of a sequence of reforms that need to be planned together? Alternatively, can the policy be broken down into a series of steps and put into place sequentially? Is it possible to alter the sequence of changes to mitigate some of the negative impacts? Would such changes or delays affect the program's success? How much flexibility do designers have in proceeding with such changes as removing subsidies on basic food commodities?

Institutional Intensity. The concept of institutional intensity is closely related to complexity. Paul reviewed World Bank sectoral loans and determined that they were "institutionally intense" if they "required organizational restructuring and policy capacity building," that is, if the policy changes require changes in organizations.[30] Some structural adjustment programs try to reform public institutions directly, greatly increasing the institutional intensity. Examples include civil service reform such as early retirement programs, dissolution of parastatals, devolution of authority from central ministries to subnational levels, and removal of price-setting authority. These have proved to be the most difficult to implement because they run counter to established roles and interests in organizations. Those planning for implementation need to anticipate that there will be major organizational and even political resistance and should map the likely sources of such resistance.

Clarity About Who Is in Charge. What units are involved in a particular activity and are they linked in any way? Most often, multiple units are involved and lines of authority are unclear. For example, in the Dominican Republic a team mapped the units in charge of formulating national agricultural policies and came up with a long list of units with few connections among them.[31] The result may be that none is in charge if the policy overlaps several units and no single unit has statutory authority. This is often the case with environmental policies that are affected by several ministries but are the responsibility of none.

MAPPING THE NEED FOR SUPPORTING SECTORAL INVESTMENTS

Nature of the Problem

The concept of a system can be a useful way to think about supporting investments. Brainstorming could identify the parts of the agricultural system, including marketing, storage, and distribution of inputs such as fertilizer, credit, research, and so forth. A historical case study could be carried out to determine which areas posed major problems. A group interested in designing more effective agricultural research, for example, could begin by conceptualizing agriculture as a "farming system" and identifying its components. Studies include individual preferences, known technology, natural resources, and community values as parts of the system that need to be linked. Research and technology, for example, need to address the actual problems that farmers face. Mapping would collect information about farmer perceptions, practices, and needs and determine whether existing research priorities matched these.[32] The mapping exercise could also examine what procedures exist for government extension workers and research units to learn about the situation of farmers, especially if they are physically remote or alienated from public programs.[33]

Mapping the Social and Political Environment

Mapping can focus either on beneficiaries or the more political concept of stakeholders. Beneficiary preferences can be mapped by asking people what they want, and needs can be mapped by asking individuals about their problems. A strategic analysis approach to improving irrigation systems in Pakistan illustrates this second alternative. The design team used members of the implementing organizations to interview farmers. Instead of asking directly about their preferences, however, they asked for information about the following: inequity of water supply; unreliability of water supply; inadequacy of water; watercourse losses; submerged outlets; use of inputs; and willingness to be involved in the system.[34] The teams then derived farmer needs from these characteristics of the water systems. Another approach to determining preferences and needs assumes that they are best revealed through an interactive strategy. Individuals may not be aware of their needs until they have a sense of options. Group discussion may provide a more accurate picture of what local people want and what their situation is like.[35]

Another approach draws on the concept of stakeholders—all groups with an ability to influence the policy either positively or negatively. The list would be specific to each policy and could include local political interests, civil servants, labor unions, international organizations, revolutionaries, opposition parties, chambers of commerce, and so forth. A SWOT analysis could be used to classify them. A similar schema listed stakeholders and then indicated what transactions one might carry out with each stakeholder group. Transactions included providing financial resources, providing physical inputs, offering political support, offering technical assistance, delivering services, and providing publicity.[36] The following variation focuses on assets:[37]

Matrix for Analyzing Assets of Stakeholders
of Policy to Privatize Agricultural Inputs

Potential Assets

Stakeholders	Financial resources	Physical inputs	Political support	Service delivery assistance
Farmer organizations				
Private businesses				
Parastatals				
Banks				
Credit unions				
Donors				
Chambers of Commerce				
NGOs				

Mapping the Capacity for Implementing Supporting Investments

Three capacities are particularly relevant: project implementation, operational procedures, and the effectiveness of the wider bureaucratic setting.

Project Implementation. Supporting activities are often funded and implemented as projects. Ministries are widely judged to have a very low capacity for implementing projects based on evidence that they are unable to spend budgeted project funds in a timely manner. Recall the point in Chapter 2, however, that such delays can be traced to a number of sources, including central government financial constraints and donor regulations. Mapping therefore needs to diagnose actual reasons for spending delays. Another problem frequently raised is the failure to take a programmatic approach to projects. Budget staff can be surveyed to determine how they evaluate projects—in terms of meeting their budget, or in terms of contributing to program goals. When faced with budget cuts, do they make these across the board or do they make programmatic judgments?

Complexity affects how supporting services are implemented. Does a proposed project, for example, prescribe a relatively simple task of delivering a specific service or a more complex task of changing behavior in a community or altering economic institutions? One mapping schema developed for the World Bank lists the following indicators of complexity: variety of services, amount of change desired, whether tasks have to be sequenced, whether the tasks are poorly defined, the scale of the services, whether the services involve new activities, and whether there are conflicting views about them.[38] The higher the score on any of these the more complex the policy, and the more flexibility will have to be incorporated in its design.

Operational Procedures. The organizational procedures of financial management, personnel, data collection, and monitoring can all be mapped.[39]

Financial management. Three points are mentioned most frequently: the use of budgeting for managing programs, the capacity to monitor government expenditures, and the adequacy of the revenue system. Mapping the revenue system involves the following variables: who pays for services, what form of payment is used, how are taxes collected, what are the sources of local revenue, what are the equity implications of revenue sources, and what is the financial relationship between central and local governments?[40]

Personnel systems. Personnel procedures continue to be one of the weakest points in many organizations. Klitgaard documents the difficulties in improving civil service systems and in rewarding good performance, given the severe shortage of resources in these systems. His concern that we have "incentive myopia"—a lack of concern with incentives—suggests the need to map incentives and the extent to which they are linked to performance measures. As an example, he notes that in Ghana the Railways Corporation "linked heavily subsidized packages of food to the achievement of measurable results for each worker and for the Corporation as a whole."[41]

Data collection and monitoring capacity. Thomas Dichter laments that development management has focused too much on interpersonal skills and overlooked the need for basic accounting systems and data analysis procedures and skills.[42] A common problem is a lack of information for determining what a project or program is accomplishing. According to Joseph Wholey, data are often collected about resources spent and activities carried out but not about outcomes. He recommends a process in which stakeholders collaborate on defining outcomes and reasonable indicators for these, including the "explicit use of multiple objectives and multiple performance indicators in defining 'good performance'; and use of qualitative as well as quantitative indicators to capture the nuances of good program performance."[43] A mapping exercise to determine whether and how results are currently assessed might look like the following:

Events   Performance Indicators   Data Sources

A matrix can be used to map the existing strengths and weaknesses for organizational procedures.

Mapping Organizational Procedures

Procedure	Description	Strengths	Weaknesses
Financial management			
Incentives for staff			
Data collection to monitor results			

Bureaucratic Setting. This factor refers to the place of the organization in the larger bureaucratic setting. Mapping could list all of the units involved in an activity—planning, implementing, collecting resources, monitoring, and evaluating. It could examine the vertical relations within a program ministry, as well as the horizontal relations with central ministries of finance and planning, and with regional organizations, field units, and local governments. Mapping would lay out the various units involved in carrying out a policy and indicate how they divide or share responsibilities among themselves and how they are related to each other.

A matrix can be designed to capture these relationships. A project unit in Cairo charged to implement a policy to decentralize the provision of urban services in that city found that overlapping authority among government agencies was very confusing and inhibiting. The implementors began by listing all of the tasks involved in carrying out urban services and all of the units of government involved in service delivery. They placed these lists on a matrix and used it in meetings with government officials to sort out relationships and identify points of tension and confusion. The following chart is excerpted from the original.[44]

Responsibility Chart

Actions	Units			
	Project Manager	City Council	Executive Council	Ministry
Project design				
Cost estimate				
Award of contract				
Inspections				

A cell was coded R if a unit had principal responsibility for an action, C if it had to be consulted, V if it had veto power.

Analyses usually find that there is inadequate coordination among different units, producing stalemates and wasted efforts. The need for coordination may be overstated, however. Leonard proposes a useful distinction that needs to be mapped. He notes that Kenya has dramatically increased its milk production even though there is little coordination among the several units. He distinguishes between components that have an "additive" effect and those that have an "interactive" effect. When two components interact so that both have to be present, then integration is important. For example, he notes that artificial insemination and dipping to control tick-borne diseases are interactive; neither would be effective without the other. In other cases, the effects are only additive, such as veterinary medicine and cattle management practices. In these cases, coordination is less essential.[45]

A common problem in bureaucratic settings is achieving a balance between accountability on the one hand and discretion to experiment and adapt on the other. Finance ministries often insert controls in the system to ensure the integrity of the funds and cope with widespread abuses. The result is a hierarchical system with little delegation of authority. In Guinea, for example, the results were paralyzing. Mapping showed that project field officers had to file sixteen different request forms for each purchase, a requirement that created excessive rigidity and explained why often nothing was done.[46]

Techniques for Collecting Information About Organizations. In "critical incidents analysis" interviewers ask practicing managers to briefly describe critical incidents that they have had to confront over the past year. Such descriptions presumably provide greater insight into the actual experiences of managers than questionnaires, which can produce vague and general responses.[47] A second technique, a flowchart, is used to ask those being interviewed to describe the steps that are taken in any process and is illustrated by the earlier example in which staff listed sixteen steps in requesting a purchase.[48]

MAPPING INSTITUTIONS

Nature of the Problem

Institutions refer to the set of organizations, norms, and rules in a policy arena. Institutional analysis begins with a policy and asks what set of institutions—public, private, or voluntary—is most appropriate for carrying it out. Since policy changes frequently require implementing units to delegate some responsibilities to other units and also to stimulate and develop stronger private sectors, institutional analysis is increasingly included in discussions of implementing policy changes. Several techniques have been developed for mapping institutional alternatives; four are described here.

Public Choice and the Demand Characteristics of Goods. Economists conceptualize policies according to the kinds of demands they elicit and then analyze which rules and organizations will provide a service or good most efficiently.[49] These assumptions, often associated with public choice theory, were described in Chapter 3. The present discussion illustrates how they have been applied in an institutional analysis of feeder roads in Bangladesh. The stated purpose was to design a package of investments in the rural road systems so that the roads would yield sufficient benefits to justify the investment. This involved three different studies in the affected communities. First, a technical study was done to map the soil conditions, the usage of the roads, feasible road surface types, available labor pool, and so forth. Second, a financial analysis was carried out. This included a cost-benefit analysis of the likely benefits from improved roads, the characteristics of the beneficiaries, the maintenance costs, the impact on land values, and the likely impact on traffic density and cost of marketing agricultural produce. The financial analysis also included a study of alternative ways to finance roads, including user fees, tax policies, and local tax administration.

The analysts followed the technical and financial studies with an institutional analysis. The purpose was to determine if there was any link between those who would benefit from a policy and those who paid for it. If such a linkage was lacking, there was little incentive to build a cost-effective road system, monitor its usage, or maintain it. They mapped how roads decisions were made, how the benefits and costs were distributed, what role the local government played, how maintenance was carried out, how contractors were supervised, and so forth. Their study of the present institutions showed severe structural biases against effective maintenance, against monitoring the engineers, and against getting the users to pay for any benefits they would receive. This mapping laid the basis for their recommendations to develop alternative institutions, including user fees and community organizations, that would counter these structural biases by connecting benefits from improved roads with payments and responsibility for maintaining them.[50]

The approach is particularly relevant when people are clear about their preferences, when efficiency is the most appropriate criterion for selecting among institutions, and when voluntary institutions are present in an area.

Historical Analysis of Institutions. Richard Nelson proposes a historical analysis to examine what institutional problems have arisen in the past in a particular policy arena.[51] He suggests the categories as an alternative to traditional economic models that map the costs and benefits associated with a policy. Nelson agrees with the economists' emphasis on responding to preferences, but he is concerned that often individuals are not well informed about a policy. Therefore, his model maps the extent to which a policy includes arrangements for informing and educating individuals as well as responding to their needs.

1. Develop a case study of a policy issue, examining what problems have arisen in the past. Specifically,
   a. Are preferences informed and expressed?
   b. Are some organizations responding?
   c. Do the organizations adjust as changes occur?
2. Compare how different policies or institutional arrangements would handle each of these questions.
3. Propose a more adequate set of institutions that would inform as well as respond to preferences.

These particular questions are useful when individuals are uninformed or unclear about their preferences and/or when preferences are changing. The model could be used to map institutions for providing health and nutrition programs or extension services. Do they inform the community and enable individuals to make more informed decisions? What are the alternative ways of providing health care and extension services, and how well would they inform the community?

Comparative Advantage. Uphoff suggests analyzing different institutions according to the economic principle of comparative advantage. He asks when local institutions are likely to be more efficient than national ones; if local institutions have an advantage, what are the comparative advantages of local agencies, local governments, membership organizations, cooperatives, service organizations, and private businesses. He suggests that local institutions will have the advantage where benefits are immediate and tangible and when policies require interdependent behavior.[52]

SWOT Analysis of Available Institutions. A fourth technique for mapping institutions uses a SWOT analysis. For example, those implementing a policy to stimulate agricultural production might decide to focus on the need for increased credit in rural areas. They could examine the following institutions for providing credit and carry out a SWOT analysis of each: state agricultural banks, credit agencies, national and regional development agencies, area pilot projects, crop-purchasing authorities, farmer associations, cooperatives, credit unions, commercial banking systems, private processors and exporters, suppliers, distributors and dealers, and village merchants.[53] Those doing a strategic analysis could review such a list, determine which are relevant to the policy at hand, and indicate the potential assets the various units could bring, the problems they are likely to have, the opportunities they present for overcoming some of the problems in the past, and the threats they offer.

Mapping the Social and Political Environment

The fourth approaches to institutional analysis described above include efforts to map the environment. One could also assess the legal framework in a country and the impact it has on the private sector. What are the effects of present regulations, and to what extent do laws give businessmen confidence in the future and thus encourage them to invest? A mapping of the private sector in Jamaica by the U.S. Government Accounting Office (GAO) illustrates the information one can produce. Following interviews with the local business community to determine why the private sector had not grown faster in Jamaica, they cited the following problem areas:

1. *Lack of confidence in private sector.* Business leaders doubted the government would carry through on policies to support them. In particular the government had been slow to carry out an export incentive program and actions to make foreign exchange more available to productive enterprises.
2. *Complex government bureaucracy.* Complex regulations discourage investments. For example, thirteen different institutions share responsibility for industrial policies, services, factory space, financial assistance, and management of publicly owned manufacturing companies.

3. *Infrastructure problems.* Power outages and water shutoffs are frequent. Even where infrastructure was adequate, maintenance was poor.

4. *Other constraints.* These include shortage of skilled workers, short-term practices of businessmen, manufacturing inefficiencies, and labor union demands.[54]

Mapping the Capacity for Implementing Alternative Institutions

Two implementation problems are noted here. First, the public sector may be wary of efforts to relinquish control to other units; second, if multiple units are used, it is often difficult to get them to cooperate in providing services.

Role of Public Sector. Institutional analysis requires a close look at the role of the public sector and frequently leads to recommendations to alter that role considerably. The example in Chapter 1, in which publicly funded research organizations distribute seed to farmers for conditioning and promote private firms to take over their production, changes the role of the organizations from providing the service itself to stimulating and encouraging other units.[55] Such changes may be threatening to individuals who have a personal, and often a monetary, stake in continuing an activity. It is well known that individuals are often loathe to make changes and that significant inducements may be needed.[56] Policy changes may also offend officials' sense of the proper role of government in a society. A mapping exercise could examine what private and voluntary organizations need from the government. Research in the United States suggests that governments are spending more time on dispensing information, keeping units abreast of new technology, and bringing units together to collaborate.[57] The need for information and assistance and the attitudes of public officials toward this evolving role could be mapped.

Cooperation Among Institutions. The question of cooperation is important because of the well-documented fact that organizations find it exceedingly hard to work together. It is important therefore to examine both what units are potentially available and what procedures and incentives might induce them to cooperate with each other. A mapping session might address the following issues: What are the formal and informal relationships among the units? What incentives exist for them to work together? Most interorganizational studies take an economic approach to organizational incentives and propose that units will work together when they need something from each other, such as resources, support, and information. One study, however, found that when organizations share the same policy goals, they are often willing to cooperate whether or not they need something from each other. Thus, the mapping exercise could collect information both about an organization's need for resources and its policy goals.[58]

MAPPING HUMAN RESOURCE NEEDS

Nature of the Problem

Increasingly, observers are urging that more resources be put into developing human resources—education, health, job training. The argument can be made on humanitarian grounds and tied to a definition of development as enhancing peoples' capacity for self-determined growth.[59] The argument can also be linked to policy reforms and economic growth. The *World Development Report 1990* proposed that improving human resources is one way to ensure that economic growth reaches all members of a society, including the poorest. Several problems have arisen, however. Severe resource shortages have led to drastic reductions in social service expenditures, and service-providing bureaucracies are frequently inefficient and unresponsive to individual needs. Mapping could determine what is being done in the education, health, nutrition, and family planning sectors; who is responsible; indicators of results in these areas; access of groups to these services, particularly the poor; and recurrent costs and cost effectiveness.

Mapping the Political and Social Environment

Two factors can be mapped here. First, data on education, health, and birth rates can be used to assess the resources and deficits among the populace. In many countries there has been marked improvements in nutrition, for example. A mapping exercise could focus particularly on successful cases and the reasons for them.[60] A second factor concerns the ways in which people earn a living. It is particularly important to survey the work patterns of the poor, since they frequently hold a variety of jobs. "It is not uncommon for different family members and the same individual to be cultivators, hunters and gatherers, small artisans, petty traders and wage laborers at various times of the year."[61] Analysts working in the Philippines, for example, decided that a traditional demographic profile of community members—income, size of family, etc.—would not give managers the kinds of information they needed to promote development in the area or assist community members. They designed a survey to determine how people actually earned a living. This kind of information would tell managers about the variety of coping strategies that community members were using. Managers could then use this information to design the policy response and involve community members in assisting with it.[62]

It is also important to determine the diversity in a community. Observers often generalize about beneficiaries and look at averages and general tendencies. In fact, there may be important variations that need to be taken into account in designing services. There may be very significant differences between the wants and needs of male and female farmers, for example, that will have a major influence on the kinds of services that are needed. Similarly, the needs of the poorest may differ from those with slightly more income. Tendler proposes dividing the poor into three groups so that information about those at the bottom is included, and Esman reminds observers to look at the special needs of the landless.[63]

A third factor to be examined is the demands and preferences for these services. In the area of primary health care, Uphoff emphasizes the need to know about community preferences for preventative versus curative programs and individuals' perceptions of the relationship between the costs and benefits of various health care measures (mosquito nets, hospitalization, sanitation, inoculations, etc.). He describes communities in Guatemala where a rural health program stressed prevention of disease, but community members wanted medical services.[64]

Mapping the Capacity for Implementing Proposed Changes

Given the rigidities in large bureaucracies and the scarcity of resources for human services, institutional alternatives need to be considered. Hence, the earlier discussion about alternative institutions is particularly applicable. Uphoff, for example, urges that those concerned with primary health care explore the variety of institutional options that exist, particularly local options. He proposes mapping the following: local offices of the Ministry of Health (range of services and outreach); local government (role in sanitation and generating revenue); voluntary organizations (linkages to community); cooperatives (access to resources for health care); service organizations (extent of community-based programs); private providers (role in delivering goods and services); and private health practitioners (midwives, paraprofessionals). Mapping would then consider which institutions are best able to perform different tasks in the health care arena.[65] They could draw on any of the four analytic strategies proposed in the previous section for analyzing institutions. Second, mapping could examine how the services are financed, whether through government funds, user fees, self-help, external contributions by future employers, and so forth.

MAPPING SOCIAL MOBILIZATION

Nature of the Problem

A concern for mobilization assumes that prices alone may not be enough to ensure that everyone, particularly the poor, will participate in economic development. Economic factors, such as access to jobs and land and fair returns for labor, are essential inducements. However, peasants, in particular, are often characterized by defeatism and alienation from government activities and lack the self-confidence necessary to undertake risks and innovations.[66] A number of observers—Hirschman, Korten, and Uphoff, for example—cite evidence that bottom-up communal organizations can energize people and stimulate them to become involved in development activities.[67] Their descriptions echo the themes in Chapter 4 on the influence of ideas, the evolving nature of preferences, and the role that institutions play in shaping preferences and stimulating behavior. Their point is that social mobilization enables the poor, particularly the more isolated rural poor, to participate in economic growth, respond to price incentives, and take advantage of investments in human resources.

Mapping the Social and Political Environment

Mapping can examine three characteristics of communities. Planners can collect information about preferences and needs as described in the last section; they can canvass the indigenous leadership in communities; and they can survey the voluntary organizations in a community. As Esman and Uphoff show in their study of local organizations, the latter are often the best mechanism for reaching the poor.[68] And Hirschman adds that past experiences with community action fosters social energy, even if earlier efforts failed. For example, a particular fishing cooperative that he visited "could only come into being through the sense of comradeship and community, the dispelling of isolation and mutual distrust that resulted from the common action taken many years before."[69]

Mapping the Capacity for Implementing Efforts to Mobilize Communities

One implementation problem is that governments are easily threatened and are unwilling to encourage mobilization unless they retain considerable control over the activities.[70] (Recall the government-led mobilization Saemaul Undong movement in South Korea, described in Chapter 1.) On the other hand, implementing officials may be willing to either tolerate or assist in organizing communities in order to gain their support and to supplement dwindling budgets.[71] A second problem is that community organizations frequently need a lot of assistance and support if they are to play a major role in mobilizing communities. According to Esman and Uphoff, based on their review of local organizations worldwide, "the problem is more a matter of sustaining LOs and making them effective than of calling them into existence."[72] A review of voluntary groups funded by USAID agreed that they

Table 7.1. Selected Issues in Diagnosing the Policy Arena

MAPPING MACRO AND SECTORAL LEVEL ECONOMIC POLICY ARENAS

Nature of the Problem

Internal and external causes of economic problems
Historical experiences and future trends
Available resources for economic investment

Mapping the Social and Political Environment

Behavior patterns and economic incentives
Winners and losers from projected reforms
Attitudes towards growth as a national strategy

Mapping the Capacity for Implementing the Reforms

Core economic instruments for managing the economy
Data collection and analysis capacity
Linkages among policy incentives
Clarity about who is in charge

MAPPING THE NEED FOR SUPPORTING SECTORAL INVESTMENTS

Nature of the Problem

Sector as a system of interdependent parts

Mapping the Social and Political Environment

Beneficiaries: preferences and needs
Stakeholders: assets and weaknesses
Resources: Finances, political support

Mapping the Capacity for Implementing Supporting Investments

Capacity for project implementation
Operational procedures: financial management, personnel system, data collection and monitoring
Effectiveness of the wider bureaucratic setting: units involved, relations among them, respective
  responsibilities, coordination and cooperation, controls and delegation

MAPPING INSTITUTIONS

Nature of the Problem

Analysis and comparison of institutional alternatives

Mapping the Social and Political Environment

Nature of existing institutions, including private sector
Legal framework for the private sector

Mapping the Capacity for Implementing Alternative Institutions

Role of public sector in assisting other organizations
Mutual needs and interests among institutions

MAPPING HUMAN RESOURCE NEEDS

Nature of the Problem

Severe resource shortages and reductions in services
Inefficiencies in service-providing bureaucracies

Mapping the Social and Political Environment

Data on education, health, nutrition, birth rates
Successes in improving education and health
Ways in which people earn a living
Preferences for services

Mapping the Capacity for Implementing Improved Services

Institutional alternatives for providing services

MAPPING SOCIAL MOBILIZATION

Nature of the Problem

Sources of social energy in the population

Mapping the Social and Political Environment

Information about preferences and needs
Indigenous leadership in communities
Potential voluntary organizations

Mapping the Capacity for Mobilizing Communities

Extent of government support for mobilization
Sources for assisting voluntary organizations

need a lot of external assistance, including training and management skills, in order to be successful.[73]

CONCLUSIONS

A key theme in strategic analysis is that some combination of policy planners, managers, stakeholders, and technical assistants needs to assess the opportunities and problems in LDC situations in order to develop effective strategies for intervening and bringing about change. This chapter has suggested a number of issues that these groups could map. It has drawn on experiences with policy reforms and pointed toward the kinds of issues that have posed problems in the past. While these are meant to be suggestive only, they do indicate ways to introduce substantive issues into the diagnosis and to build on the cumulative experiences in LDCs. The discussion also posed the issues in the form of new concepts and matrices in order to stimulate participants to shake loose from a status quo mindset and to engage others with alternative views.

NOTES

1. Lindenberg and Crosby, 1981, *Managing Development*, 27.
2. Mitroff and Emshoff, 1979, "Strategic Assumption Making"; Patton, 1986, *Utilization-Focused Evaluation*.
3. See Chambers, 1980, *Rural Poverty*.
4. Chambers, 1980, *Rural Poverty*. A growing literature discusses sector-specific ways to carry out rapid reconnaissance. See, for example, Scrimshaw and Hurtado, 1987, *Rapid Assessment*.
5. Honadle, 1982, "Rapid Reconnaissance."
6. See Bryson, 1988, *Strategic Planning*.
7. Bryson, 1988, *Strategic Planning*.
8. The following authors develop similar matrices: Brinkerhoff, 1990, *Development Program Performance*; Paul, 1982, *Managing Development Programs*; Rondinelli, et al., 1989, "Contingency Planning."
9. White, 1986, *Managing Development*, 40.
10. Paul, 1989, "Institutional Reforms"; Vondal, 1987, "A Review"; Heaver and Israel, 1986, *Country Commitment*; Rondinelli, et al., 1989, "Contingency Planning," 48.
11. Ansoff, et al., 1976, *Strategic Planning*; Smith, et al., 1980, *Design of Organizations*.
12. Korten, 1980, "Community Organization."
13. Macadam, et al., 1989, *Strategic Planning*, 22.
14. Bienen and Waterbury, 1989, "Privatization," 618.
15. A World Bank publication traces this disagreement: World Bank, 1988, *Adjustment Lending*, 58.
16. World Bank, 1990, *World Bank Development Report 1990*, Ch. 1.

17. Streeten, 1987, "Structural Adjustment."

18. Kaufman, 1989, "Politics," 409.

19. Kaufman, 1989, "Politics," 410.

20. Mittleman, 1988, *Underdevelopment.*

21. See 1988 amendments to Handbooks 3 and 4 on project design by the Agency for International Development.

22. Kaufman, 1989, "Politics," 407–409.

23. J. Nelson, 1984, "Political Economy," 994. The maxim about political dynamics in LDCs is based on Bates, 1981, *Markets and States.* Frameworks for mapping the political arena can also be found in Ilchman and Uphoff, 1969, *Political Economy,* Chapters 1 and 2; Lindenberg and Crosby, 1981, *Managing Development,* Chapter 2.

24. Lindenberg, 1989, "Economic Adjustment."

25. Johnson, 1987, "Political Institutions." See also the case study of Indonesia in the World Bank series *The Political Economy of Poverty, Equity and Growth,* forthcoming.

26. Nicholas, 1988, *World Bank's Lending,* 23.

27. Kaufman, 1989, "Politics," 408.

28. White, 1990a, "Implementing."

29. Church and Castro, 1988, *Agricultural Policy,* 3, 4.

30. Paul, 1989, "Institutional Reforms," 22.

31. Church and Castro, 1988, "Agricultural Policy," 2.

32. White, 1990c, "Agricultural Research."

33. Chambers, 1980, *Rural Poverty.*

34. Jones and Clyma, 1986, "Management Improvement," 19.

35. Korten, 1980, "Community Organization."

36. Brinkerhoff and Hopkins, 1989, "Institutional Dimensions."

37. Austin and Ickis, 1986, "Management," describe how the private sector was viewed as an asset by the socialist regime in Nicaragua.

38. Brinkerhoff and Hopkins, 1989, "Institutional Dimensions."

39. See Kiggundu, 1989, *Managing Organizations;* Diallo, et al., 1988, "Organization Development"; Kettering, 1987, *Microcomputer;* Paul, 1983, *Strategic Management.*

40. Rondinelli, et al., 1989, "Analyzing Decentralization," 70–72.

41. Klitgaard, 1989, "Incentive Myopia."

42. Dichter, 1987, *Development Management.*

43. Wholey, 1983, *Evaluation,* 6, 16, 45.

44. *Neighborhood Urban Services Project Evaluation,* Phase II, Washington, D.C.: International Science and Technology Institute, 1986, 9.

45. Leonard, 1989, *African Governance,* 293. A useful discussion of coordination problems is found in Honadle and VanSant, 1985, *Implementation.*

46. Diallo, et al., 1988, "Organization Development."

47. A team used this technique in southern Africa to develop a revealing profile of the actual behavior of managers at different levels. Montgomery, 1986a. "Bureaucratic Politics"; 1986b, "Life at the Apex."

48. Wholey, 1983, *Evaluation;* Patton, 1981, *Creative Evaluation.*

49. For a particularly useful set of studies on common goods problems in the development context, see the essays collected by the National Research Council, 1986, *Common Property.*

50. Associates in Rural Development, 1989, *Bangladesh.*

51. R. Nelson, 1977, *Moon and Ghetto.*

52. Uphoff, 1986, *Local Institutional Development,* 17–18.

53. This list was adapted from Gonzalez-Vega, 1979, *Invierno*, 8. See also Mosley, 1986, "Agricultural Performance."

54. General Accounting Office (GAO) report on U.S. assistance to Jamaica, GAO/ID-83-45, April 1983.

55. See Austin and Ickis study of Nicaragua for an example, 1986, "Management."

56. For example, Heaver, 1982, *Bureaucratic Politics*.

57. White, 1989, "Public Management."

58. J. Weiss, 1987, "Pathways," makes this argument and also reviews the literature on cooperation as exchange.

59. Korten, 1987, "Third Generation."

60. World Bank, 1990, *World Development Report 1990*, Ch. 2.

61. World Bank, 1990, *World Development Report 1990*, 2.30 of draft version.

62. Korten and Carner, 1984, "Planning Frameworks." Patton, 1981, *Creative Evaluation*, also discusses the value of asset analysis.

63. Tendler, 1982, *Private Voluntary Organizations*, and Esman, 1978, *Landlessness*, distinguish among different types of poverty.

64. Uphoff, 1986, *Local Institutional Development*, 92–101.

65. Uphoff, 1986, *Local Institutional Development*, 82–109.

66. Mittleman, 1988, *Underdevelopment*, 159–168.

67. Korten, 1980, "Community Organization"; Uphoff, 1987, "Social Energy"; Hirschman, 1984, *Getting Ahead*.

68. Esman and Uphoff, 1984, *Local Organizations*, 58–82.

69. Hirschman, 1988, "Social Energy," 14.

70. Esman and Uphoff, 1984, *Local Organizations*, 36.

71. Korten, 1980, "Community Organization," describes how the National Irrigation Administration in the Philippines mobilized community organizations.

72. Esman and Uphoff, 1984, *Local Organizations*, 35.

73. Huntington, 1987, *Institutional Development*.

8

Identifying Strategic Issues

ISSUES PRIOR TO STRATEGIES

Although it is possible to move directly from mapping to designing a strategy for carrying out a policy, there is value in an intermediary step in which participants identify those particular issues that appear to be most critical and that they intend to tackle first. A strategic issue refers to a basic policy choice and, according to John Bryson, identifying such issues "is the heart of the strategic planning process" since it determines how strategies will be framed and carried out. He continues that the process can generate tensions. "Identifying strategic issues typically is one of the most riveting steps for participants in strategic planning. Virtually every strategic issue involves conflicts: what will be done, why it will be done, how it will be done, when it will be done, where it will be done, who will do it, and who will be advantaged or disadvantaged by it. These conflicts may draw people together or pull them apart, but in either case participants will feel heightened emotion and concern."[1]

The literature on strategic planning proposes a number of reasons for identifying this as a separate step.[2]

First, it encourages *selectivity* and helps people focus on what is most important. Since officials cannot do everything, they need to prioritize issues for the short and long range.

Second, it ensures that implementors *focus on problem situations and not solutions.* This emphasis on issues encourages participants to select strategies that focus on particular uncertainties or problem areas, rather than select them because they are easy or routine. The discussion of structured techniques in Chapter 5 also emphasized the value of separating issues from solutions. When these are not separated, it is too easy to adopt steps that look relatively easy to put in place, or that fit existing norms and biases but do not necessarily help people cope with the most critical issues. A report of a strategic planning process used in Pakistan stressed this point. The models they introduced were designed to focus on "what needs to be done, not how to do it. This is the greatest asset of the models as it is all too common for people to argue about how to do something without any shared understanding of what the action is supposed to achieve."[3]

Third, identifying issues as a separate step encourages *learning by doing* or *action research*. Managers have a greater chance of improving implementation if they work on issues that are immediate to them and that they have identified as important.[4]

Fourth, it encourages *areas of common agreement*. Even if participants do not agree on objectives, they may agree on issues or on definitions of problem situations.

DEFINING ISSUES

Participants can move directly from the mapping exercises to identify the issues and then prioritize them. Alternatively, if there is agreement on goals, they could begin with goals and objectives and review them in light of discussions during the mapping stage. Ideally, issues will be stated as questions that have more than one answer. Examples of strategic issues developed in some of the cases referred to throughout this book include the following: How can the government stimulate more resources for investment, both internally and externally? How can the government reduce the flight of capital from the country? How can the Finance Ministry dispense funds to local units in a timely and efficient manner that both gives them some discretion and holds them accountable? How can marketing services be made more efficient and effective? What actions are needed to stimulate increased agricultural productivity in staples? How can training institutes improve the effectiveness of local organizations? How can a Ministry of Agriculture encourage the development and distribution of seed that is appropriate to different regions of a country?

Issues and major questions are not necessarily obvious. A group discussing a credit program could focus on how to increase general access to credit in rural areas. Alternatively, it could focus on increasing credit for poor farmers. The two questions are not the same. A program designed to move more credit to rural areas might target the better-off farmers and make no provision for poorer farmers who pose greater risks for lending institutions. Alternative ways of stating issues can come out of the mapping process described in the last chapter; they can come out of an awareness of implementation difficulties; or they can come from analytic frameworks such as those proposed for carrying out institutional analysis.

The analysis of rural roads in Bangladesh discussed in the last chapter illustrates alternative ways to define issues. The report noted that roads are typically defined as an engineering issue, and indeed an effective roads system is partially a technical issue. It is also partly a problem in understanding the social and environmental setting, and learning the kinds of roads the community needs. Third, the roads pose a financial issue, namely how to finance them. Finally, roads pose an institutional issue. How can designers ensure that those who benefit from the roads will have an incentive to contribute resources and assist in maintaining them?[5]

As another example, a ministry charged with reducing its staff can define the issues it confronts in several ways. It could state a strategic issue as, How can the agency reduce the number of staff? An alternative question would read, What personnel policy will enable the agency to match staffing with agency functions? Yet another question would ask, What can the agency do to stimulate alternative employment opportunities for staff in the private sector? The first is an immediate response to a policy mandate. The second and third formulations interpret the policy mandate in light of agency functions and political demands for job security and are able to take into account a variety of issues that would likely have arisen during the mapping sessions.

CRITERIA FOR SELECTING MAJOR ISSUES

1. Identify the major issues that arose during the mapping exercises —both substantive and institutional.
2. Select issues where interventions can make a difference, where new policies, leadership, or effective management can change the situation.
3. Select issues where there is a possibility of changing views—both core and secondary views.

Identify Major Problem Areas

Two kinds of issues arise in thinking about policy reforms: substantive issues related to economic development, and capacity issues for designing and carrying out selected strategies. If lack of credit is identified as a critical substantive issue, then it is also important to ask what institutional problems have arisen in making credit available in rural areas. Reviewing the mapping exercise, participants can ask, Is the credit failure due to a lack of available funds, a lack of organizations for processing the loans, a lack of guarantees for loan defaults, or a lack of confidence by the business community that farmers will respond to new incentives?

Some issues involve a general capacity in an organization and are not unique to a specific policy. An analysis of financial management procedures in the agriculture ministry in Guinea identified a number of severe problems in the management process: multiple and conflicting budgets, financial allocations that reflect available revenue rather than budget requests, a severe lack of budgeting skills, delayed disbursements, a lack of information on personnel for rewarding performance, and a lack of basic office equipment.[6] A session to identify strategic issues would translate these into questions such as: How can the budgets be rationalized and simplified? How can the process of making financial allocations be more responsive to requests? Those suggesting each issue would specify why it is important and what will happen if it is not addressed. Then the group could rank them, either through discussion or through a structured process such as the nominal group process described in Chapter 5. Presumably one would rank them according to their importance. The group could also select one of the less critical issues to gain some experience in resolving conflicts before turning to more difficult ones.

A plan for the agricultural sector in Morocco sponsored by the World Bank identified several organizational issues. A number of working groups composed of Bank staff and Moroccan counterparts carried out studies of the sector. As a result of several dialogue sessions, they identified a number of institutional capacity issues, including "lack of managerial and financial autonomy, lack of staff capacity, skills and incentives both for policy planning and service delivery." Using this analysis they moved on to the strategy planning stage in which they divided the organizational changes into several parts and designed a way to introduce them in stages. They began with a low-cost pilot program to strengthen the extension service in twenty-eight rainfed areas, with plans to expand it later.[7]

A study of reform experiences in Brazil, Argentina, and Mexico identified major issues that covered two dimensions—internal and external problems, and substantive and implementation problems. Kaufman noted that the major internal problem was political opposition to austerity and increased taxes. The two internal implementation problems concerned a poor capacity for data analysis and the limited authority in central finance ministries. The major external problem was the debt drain and the power of external creditors to control access to capital.[8]

Make a Difference

Identify issues where policy changes can make a difference and where implementors can expect to have *some influence or control*. For example, implementors can ask whether the content of the policy can be adjusted, or what opportunities there are for developing new organizational units.[9] If implementors can identify a few areas where they can be certain of making a difference early in the process, they may be able to use these experiences to give them some confidence and experience to tackle more difficult issues later.

Influence Beliefs

Implementors need to consider opportunities to *change or alter the setting, including peoples' beliefs*, to be proactive, rather than simply adapt to preferences. For example, if intended beneficiaries are not interested in a particular policy change, the important issue may be changing their minds or learning more about their needs rather than simply adapting to their lack of interest.[10] Participants need to look for opportunities where their group or separate individuals can exert some leadership and make changes rather than accept the prevailing conditions.[11]

TECHNIQUES FOR DEFINING AND SELECTING ISSUES

Defining Issues Based on Mapping Exercises

Discussions can build on the earlier mapping discussions and the analyses of existing problems and situations. Group process techniques described earlier can be helpful at this stage. Whereas mapping can generate information, the task here is to synthesize and focus efforts. Techniques for synthesizing different views, however, are less fully developed than techniques for generating options. Recall that one of the procedures described in Chapter 5 suggested that a small team might develop a set of issues as a "straw man" to give the group something to focus on and revise.

One report of a strategic process suggests the following procedure for identifying issues.[12] Individuals begin by writing answers to three questions: What is the issue? What factors make it a strategic issue? What are the consequences of failing to deal with it?

Participants are given time to identify these, perhaps as much as a week, after which they come together in a joint planning session. The separate issues are posted visibly for all to see and discuss. A two-by-two matrix can be used to compare them, using a SWOT analysis, with strengths and weaknesses posed by each issue on one dimension and opportunities and threats on the other.

	Strengths	Weaknesses
Opportunities	Opportunities for taking advantage of strengths	Opportunities for overcoming weaknesses
Threats	Threats to realizing these strengths	Threats that make it hard to overcome weaknesses

Participants can use the matrix to analyze and compare the issues. Those cases where an issue is associated with many items under strengths and opportunities can be tentatively proposed as the strategic issue and then discussed further.

Identifying Issues Without a Mapping Exercise

Sometimes external groups can assist in identifying issues, as in the following cases: In 1986 the Science and Technology (S & T) Bureau within USAID asked missions to identify specific issues for which the Washington office might provide assistance in promoting policy reforms. To stimulate a dialogue, the Bureau reviewed mission documents and for each country identified those issues that seemed to stand out as most important. The Bureau presented the proposed issues to the mission staffs in order to initiate a dialogue in an upcoming visit to the country. This procedure illustrates a promising technique for identifying priority issues when a conscious mapping event has not been carried out. The following summary of two of their efforts to define issues shows how the documents from two different countries posed very different sets of priority issues.

Guatemala. General issue: Public sector deficits and declining revenues. Specific issues: (1) How do interest groups assess the risks and uncertainties of different reform measures and what is their likely success rate? (2) What role can the political leadership play in a "national dialogue" and "what means exist for leaders to promote popular and elite understanding of proposed changes in tax structures?" (3) How can the government improve its capacity to reform and administer the tax system? This last question posed a number of additional, more technical issues: How can the tax system be improved to be more elastic and efficient? How can the government collect better data for making better revenue projections and estimates of capital flight? Which sectors should receive priority in investments? How can Guatemala's domestic tax system be accommodated with the region's common market?

Costa Rica. General issue: Divestiture of state-owned enterprises (SOEs). Specific issues: (1) How can support be built for divestiture? "What steps must be taken to ease adjustment, raise public knowledge of SOE losses and build popular support for reduction of the public sector involvement?" (2) What financial mechanisms can be developed to restructure SOE debt, such as financing the write-offs of SOE losses and gaining a better understanding of credit requirements? (3) How can the government determine the long-term developmental needs of the private sector, including needed managerial and technical skills and fiscal and legal constraints?

Note that the proposed issues included problems related to the political setting and to the capacity for implementing the reforms. They also illustrate how one can identify fairly general issues and then break them down into more specific ones.

CONCLUSIONS

Identifying issues is an important step in a strategic process because it focuses participants on problem areas rather than on solutions. The examples illustrate that issues can be identified in a number of ways besides a formal planning process—including case studies and a review of documents. To assist in a strategic process, however, issues need to emerge out of an understanding of particular situations and then be fed back to officials, managers, and stakeholders for their response. They need to be relevant to the situation and owned by the participants.

NOTES

1. Bryson, 1988, *Strategic Planning*, 139.
2. This discussion draws heavily from Bryson, 1988, *Strategic Planning*.
3. Macadam, et al., 1989, *Strategic Planning*, 9.
4. Kettering, 1985, *Action-Training;* Mickelwait, 1980, *Technical Assistance;* Brinkerhoff and Ingle, 1989, Structured Flexibility."
5. Associates in Rural Development, 1989, *Bangladesh*, 18ff.
6. Diallo, et al., 1988, "Organization Development"; Brinkerhoff and Goldsmith, 1988, "Administrative Reform"; Klitgaard, 1989, "Incentive Myopia."
7. Paul, 1989, *Institutional Reforms*, 20–21.
8. Kaufman, 1989, "Politics."
9. Smith, et al., 1980, *Design of Organizations*.
10. Paul, 1983, *Strategic Management*.
11. Leonard, 1987, "Political Realities."
12. Bryson, 1988, *Strategic Planning*, 149ff.

9

Strategies to Cope
with Major Issues

CHARACTERISTICS OF STRATEGIES

Strategies vary according to who is involved and whether participants are discussing a broad policy framework or a more specific implementation plan. Strategies include recommendations about the policy itself, about its timing and content, as well as implementation activities that address problems or issues identified earlier. They can be designed to mobilize stakeholders and gain their support, or to build coalitions among political interests. They can include compensations for opponents, actions to divert the opposition or to coopt political leaders, and sequencing decisions to buy support.[1] Policy reform experiences suggest that appropriate strategies have four characteristics: they are based on earlier mapping and issue identification exercises; they propose innovations; they link immediate steps to a broader plan or program; and they stimulate an organizational capacity for implementation and learning. First, strategies are based on the information produced during the mapping exercises, particularly on the strengths and opportunities identified in any SWOT analyses that were carried out. They also suggest how to deal with the questions posed by strategic issues.

Second, strategies involve innovation and creative thinking. According to the International Labor Organization (ILO), "not every planning for three, five or more years ahead deserves to be called strategic. If mere extrapolation is used to produce a plan instead of creative thinking based on thorough analysis of facts, or if analysis is overdone but does not help to find and take new opportunities, such planning cannot normally be considered strategic."[2] For example, if the issue is to increase resources to stimulate the private sector, participants need to speculate about and compare a variety of options such as debt conversion, free trade zones, venture capital, and the establishment of market towns—in addition to more traditional activities such as offering extended credit. Planning sessions, therefore, need to include conceptual exercises to stimulate new ways of thinking about an issue. According to Bryson, there has to be a catharsis stage in which participants break through their attachments to existing ways of doing things.[3]

Third, strategies need to be connected to broader programmatic concerns. Strategy decisions, therefore, will be made at both top and lower levels. Guidelines, established at the top, can provide direction.[4] At the same time, many decisions will be made lower down in the organization. Again according to Bryson, "Overall strategic guidance is given at the top, but detailed strategy formulation and implementation typically occur deeper in the organization."[5] Finally, strategies are linked to an organizational learning process. The level of uncertainty associated with collaborative implementation means that specific objectives will always have to be adjusted. Strategies, therefore, are part of an organizational learning process and need to be linked to procedures that institutionalize strategic analysis and make it a habit. They are probably best conceived as ways to cope with problems in an innovative and continuing manner, rather than simply as particular steps to solve a problem. They also need to be linked to institutions that mobilize support for policies, generate resources to continue them, and establish management systems to adapt them.[6] As David Korten puts it, the most appropriate strategy in the long run is to develop a strategic organization.[7]

FORMULATING STRATEGIES

Strategies can assume different forms. A formal written plan may be useful to help people keep track of what they are able to accomplish, but it is not essential. Bryson proposes the following steps, but insists that the thinking and analysis are more important than specific and formal plans.[8]

1. *Identify alternatives for dealing with the issue.* For example, participants planning a new activity could compare actions to establish new organizations, turn over responsibilities to the private sector, and provide price incentives to stimulate new behavior.

2. *Enumerate barriers to these.* Typical barriers relevant to the above options include rigidity within organizations, unwillingness to share information or power, lack of trained personnel, lack of incentives to encourage responsiveness, lack of appropriate information, lack of resources, and political opposition.

3. *Propose how to deal with the barriers.* Possible options to overcome organizational rigidity include providing training, exercising leadership, consulting with additional groups, and developing linkages with local organizations.

4. *Propose longer-range actions and specific steps to be taken in the*

next few months. Strategies need to include both longer-range plans and more immediate steps. Criteria for actions include technical feasibility, political acceptability, and agreement with core values.

5. *Develop a vision of success to guide implementation.* It is often helpful to have participants speculate about what a successful operation or policy would look like. What can they reasonably expect to happen? What would be different? Visions can cut through the tendency to assume that change is not possible, that the status quo is inevitable.

CONCEPTUAL EXERCISES

Conceptualizing alternatives can help participants explore innovations and resist moving to conclusions too readily. Contingency theory—the theory that strategies should be designed according to the nature of the task and the characteristics of the environment—is a particularly useful conceptual tool.[9] A report of a strategic planning effort in Pakistan illustrates such a technique. The participants were connected to an agricultural university and were considering how to improve the university's capacity for research to make the research more relevant to farmer needs. The group leaders began by making two distinctions: between an active and reflective task and between an external and internal view of the environment. This conceptualization produced the following matrix:

Approach to Task	View of Environment	
	Internal	External
Active	Mechanical	Adaptive
Reflective	Reactive	Interactive

The four types of strategies identified in the cells were then described and used to stimulate the group to think analytically about their options. A *mechanical* strategy proposes a plan of action for carrying out specific tasks, with little reflection about the skills or the larger environment. An example would be training students to speak English. An *adaptive* strategy is also active at the expense of learning, but it focuses on dealing with problems in the larger environment. An example would be a decision by farmers to cultivate larger plots of land based on increased market demand. A *reactive* strategy is designed to enhance learning, but the focus is on internal operations. An example is a rural credit bank that changes its procedures for making loans and sets up a new training course for lending officers. An *interactive* strategy emphasizes learning about the external setting. "One example is an ongoing university dialogue with outside client groups to identify groups expected to hire university graduates in the short-run, and adjust university curriculum to make graduates more attractive to potential employers in these emerging areas."[10] Participants considered these and applied them to the issue they were considering. Eventually they designed a strategy to establish a think tank to advise university officials about agriculture and research on an ongoing basis, and to monitor and evaluate what was being done.

This conceptual technique is based on a more general contingency model that stimulates participants to consider the uncertainty associated with a problem issue—uncertainty about steps to take and probable results. Some refer to the "analyzability" of the policy, "the extent to which planners can specify precisely the objectives of a task and the extent to which they can predict its impact."[11] While policies vary in their specificity as noted in Chapter 1, policy reforms have fairly low "analyzability" in this sense. Stout proposes a matrix that combines this characteristic with the extent of agreement about the goals of the policy. He uses it in a contingency analysis to suggest what kind of implementation strategy fits with each set of characteristics.[12]

Knowledge About How to Carry Out	Value Premises in Policy	
	Agree	Disagree
Certain	1. Programmed	3. Negotiated
Uncertain	2. Pragmatic	4. Chaos

Cell 1, with certain knowledge about what to do and agreement on the goals of the policy, allows for programmed decisions where tasks can be predefined and controls put in place. In Cell 2, where there is also agreement but a lack of certainty about how to proceed, implementors will need to be pragmatic and experimental. Cell 3, with certain knowledge and disagreement, calls for participants to negotiate about the content of the policy so they can proceed to carry it out. Cell 4, where there is no agreement and no certainty about what to do, Stout calls "chaos." One could argue that it is precisely in these cases that a process approach is most useful. It provides an occasion for dealing with disagreements and for designing pragmatic ways to experiment and collect more information about the impact of different strategies.

Israel suggests a similar technique for conceptualizing alternative strategies. His schema divides a wide range of activities into those that are more and less specific. He proposes an index of specificity/complexity composed of eight elements: (1) whether objectives can be defined, (2) whether methods can be defined, (3) whether controls are possible, (4) how long these characteristics hold true before they have to be modified, (5) intensity of effects on people, (6) time it takes to see effects, (7) spread of the benefits, and (8) traceability of the effects. The higher the score, the more specific a strategy can be, the more precise the objectives can be, the more discipline that can be imposed on implementors, and the more structured implementation can be. For lower scores, as is true for people-oriented projects, highly structured strategies are less appropriate. For example, policies to stimulate rainfed and irrigated agriculture score on the eight factors listed above as follows:

Rainfed agriculture—4, 3, 3, 2, 3, 2, 4, 2. Total 23.

Irrigated agriculture—4, 4, 4, 3, 4, 4, 3, 4. Total 30.

The numbers 2 and 4 for the last category indicate that it is easier to trace the effects of policy efforts to improve irrigated agriculture (4) than is the case for rainfed agriculture (2).[13] Strategies to deal with issues in the latter circumstances will need to be more open-ended and experimental.

Earlier discussions of institutional analysis illustrate the use of economic theories to conceptualize alternative models and institutional responses. Consider policy changes in the environmental policy arena. Economists generally criticize regulatory approaches because they discourage technological innovation and they require regulators to collect and analyze extensive amounts of information. They propose alternative strategies based on market forces in which regulators set targets, such as allowable amounts of pollution. Units have an incentive to select the most efficient strategy, and those units that can do so at the least cost will be motivated to do the most.[14]

Public choice theory can be used to compare alternative strategies and their appropriateness for different policies.[15] Participants would first list the institutional options that emerged from their mapping exercises. (Options include, for example: private businesses, informal sector enterprises, contracting arrangements, private voluntary organizations, membership organizations, public enterprises, self-help groups, and market surrogates.) Second, they would develop appropriate criteria for comparing these options. Public choice theory proposes responsiveness and efficiency. Equity could be chosen as an additional criterion. As a third step, participants would examine the implications of institutional changes for the role of government in this more complex policy arena. It may be necessary to facilitate and monitor these other units, bring different parties together for negotiations, and provide up-to-date information on new technology.[16] Governing bodies, in effect, would play a trade association role, assisting others to perform tasks.[17]

Participants could also conceptualize alternative strategies for paying for new initiatives. Again the procedure would be to conceptualize alternatives, develop criteria for comparing them, and identify the role of government in collecting and/or monitoring the funds. Gruber and Mohr propose a matrix to conceptualize strategies according to whether they provide social benefits and offer financial returns.[18]

and offer financial returns.[18]

Financial Returns	Social Benefits	
	Low	High
Positive	Sustain service	Expand cautiously
Negative	Discontinue	Nurture service

Services that provide low benefits and negative financial returns are too often continued to the detriment of other more valuable services. The matrix helps to make useful distinctions.

MANAGERIAL LEADERSHIP

Those who write about strategic approaches often emphasize the value of leadership, an emphasis that coincides with the literature on managers in general and development management in particular.[19] Observers note that leadership is important in situations characterized by economic chaos and scarce resources,[20] when innovation is needed, and when responsibility is dispersed among a number of units.[21] Strategies can encourage individual leaders. At the same time, it is important not to overlook leadership as a shared characteristic within a group or organization.[22]

Elmore suggests a useful metaphor for thinking about managerial leadership—managers are those who manage the "seams of government," the points where different units relate to each other.[23] According to this concept, managers need to learn to be more effective in negotiating among the different parties who influence policy implementation—other agencies, clientele groups, political groups, donors, private firms and nonprofit organizations, for example. He continues that "working the seams" involves four sets of skills. First, managers need to master the *technical core* of knowledge in their fields, including both analytic and management skills. These include competency in data collection and analysis and also in monitoring and managing people in the organization. Second, managers need to master the *institutional setting* of their work in order to organize staff most effectively and to develop linkages with other organizations. Third, managers need to be knowledgeable about the *substantive aspects* of the policy they are implementing and able to form working alliances with key groups. Fourth, managers need to develop skills in various *modes of influence*, which include communicating and negotiating with others as well as motivating them through leadership.

LEARNING ABOUT RESULTS

Strategies need to include procedures that enable implementing staff and policymakers to learn from experiences, in particular to ensure that information

First, can the implementation process be designed as a series of pilots and experiments? The point is to be willing to make mistakes, even to "embrace error," and to systematically learn from experience. Paul describes how the National Dairy Development Board of India was originally charged to develop dairy farming, fisheries, and other agricultural activities. The Board, however, decided to focus initially on dairy development and only later did it take up oil seeds development. Similarly, the National Food and Agricultural Council of the Philippines, charged with developing a number of different crops, decided to focus initially on improving rice, the country's staple food. "The intention was to reduce complexity by first focusing on a single or dominant goal and *sequentially* moving towards other goals. It was the careful attention given to the environment and the objectives laid down by the Government that led the programme leadership to this strategic choice of a dominant operating goal."[25] These steps are consistent with the organizational learning process proposed by Korten: develop a pilot project, improve its efficiency, then replicate it elsewhere.[26] In a more recent study he proposes that smaller, nongovernmental units may be useful in experimenting with different implementation strategies and then communicating that learning to government agencies.[27]

Second, whether or not implementation is broken down into a series of experimental steps, procedures are needed to collect and use data. Selecting performance measures can be critical and are usually best done in close consultation with those who will be carrying out an activity. Monitoring and evaluation also need to be ongoing activities that feed pertinent information into management decisions. For this reason, those responsible for information systems need to collaborate with implementors and be certain they collect information that those responsible for an activity will find useful. There are two reasons: the information is less apt to be irrelevant, and it is more apt to be used. Evaluators, therefore, play a facilitative and consultative role, or in Patton's words "act-react-adapt" to the needs of stakeholders, and managers play an active role in defining their needs and perceptions.

Third, policymakers need to learn about the results of the policy and encouraged to review goals and objectives periodically. Their needs may vary from the information that implementors need on a daily basis, but it can be critically important for longer-range adjustments in policy goals.

Fourth, strategies should include improved procedures for reporting and using the information, for linking it to management processes and to decisions that need to be made.[28]

CASE STUDY OF A STRATEGIC INQUIRY PROCESS

The following case describes a reportedly successful effort to use a collaborative policy inquiry process to develop a strategy for the agricultural sector in Sri Lanka.[29] The country had come close to achieving self-sufficiency in rice, and officials wanted to take a fresh look at the agricultural sector. The post-1977 government also wanted to reduce the role of the state and increase that of the private sector. Nine large and complex ministries are involved in agricultural policy, each with a number of different entitities, some with their own budgets and considerable autonomy. Prior efforts to streamline and rationalize the number of agencies had met strong political opposition. The government, encouraged by USAID, was interested in identifying both the obstacles and opportunities in long-range food and nutrition policies in order to define "priority policy changes and investment opportunities."

Planning the Process

A major decision in the planning process was selecting the agency to coordinate the strategy. Top officials compared several units. The Ministry of Plan Implementation was rejected, since most ministries retained the power to set their own investment priorities. The research unit within the Agriculture Ministry was rejected because it would have a hard time coordinating units at the same level in other ministries. The government finally selected the National Planning Division (NPD) within the Ministry of Finance and Planning. Presumably other ministries would accept its leadership, since its approval was needed for new investments and projects. The government then reviewed the relevant units to see which should participate; eight ministries were selected. All eight were required to participate actively in designing the strategy. A task force was established within each of the ministries to produce a development strategy for its subsector (irrigation, food crops, livestock, smallholder coconut, for example). Each task force had a high-ranking official assigned as a convener.

A long-term adviser was appointed to serve as a technical resource, to advise on appropriate analytic tools, to help the NPD integrate the work of the task forces and supporting studies into an overall strategy, and, finally, to serve as a resource for a range of policy and program options. His most important work was helping each task force define the purpose and scope for the subsector review and strategy document. Various short-term experts were brought in to help with special studies—rural credit, agricultural pricing, the export potential of rice, among others. They worked with local counterparts who pulled together background studies. The planners decided that each ministry would analyze its own subsector and that these studies would be incorporated into a report. The design was to take place over a two-year period and subsector reports were due in six months. Several interministerial workshops were also planned to deal with issues such as research and pricing that cut across ministries.

A three-day workshop began the process. It introduced the purpose of the process and provided an occasion for discussing the analytic approach to be used. The workshop identified several areas where the separate task forces would work together because of their overlapping data requirements. Members also identified the kinds of expertise and additional special studies they needed.

The Mapping Process

The task forces met regularly, often bringing together members of diverse units within the larger ministries. Senior decisionmakers were also routinely included. They mapped the issues in their subsectors, identified issues, and proposed strategies.

Identifying Major Issues

The reports were submitted to the NPD for review, with the goal of reaching a consensus about the major issues and proposed reforms between the NPD and the line ministry involved. A report was released and presented to a wider audience in two different workshops.

Designing Policy Strategies and Implementation Plans

A policy-level workshop brought together senior decisionmakers of the ministries to discuss the report and agree on agricultural sector policy reforms. A second technical-level workshop was then held; both analysts and decisionmakers attended and developed strategies to implement the policy issues. "To prevent the action plans from becoming overly ambitious, the analysts and decisionmakers had to set priorities and define concretely how the recommendations would be carried out. The action plans became the basis for the government's Public Investment Programme and also identified areas where foreign technical assistance was needed." Examples of selected strategies include: (1) "*Revise investment priorities.* Reduce emphasis on the largest irrigation development project, which was absorbing close to fifty percent of the government's development expenditures, and accelerate other agricultural production activities." (2) "Design programs and projects *to reform the rural credit structure*, integrating the formal and informal channels of credit." (3) "*Change the rice marketing system.* Further reduce the role of the government marketing agency and promote private trade through special credit lines for product disposal." These and other action plans continue to be used to direct budgets, plans, and investments. They are being included in the self-help plans associated with the PL-480 Title I agreement and in the government's public investment programs.

The evaluation identified the following positive results:

1. Whereas analysts usually spent all of their time compiling statistics, this process led them to analyze those issues that senior decisionmakers had identified as most important and strengthened the analytical work of the technical core.

2. The task forces brought together people from diverse parts of the ministries. "One of the problems of these large cumbersome institutions is that there are few incentives to resolve differences of opinion and arrive at a consensus on new directions. The Strategy exercise revealed to each ministry that they had the capacity to make these changes."

3. "The Strategy exercise clearly improved the working relations between decisionmakers and analysts. In the workshops the senior decisionmakers were brought together with analysts to develop the action plans. Over a three-day period, they worked together in groups of six or seven people to make policy and programmatic decisions. This sort of working relationship rarely, if ever, takes place in the normal working environment of these ministries."

4. The process highlighted the deficiencies in the agricultural planning capacities in the ministry and participants were very open to a proposed project for improving their analytic capacity.

5. "The Strategy succeeded in promoting a great deal of interaction among participating ministries. Technical officers working in the different ministries seldom have the opportunity to look beyond their own ministry's area of concern. What is more, outside officials do not usually discuss actions and policies with the technical officer of another ministry. The Strategy's use of task forces and workshops made this possible and exposed analysts to concerns and issues that transcended their own ministries."

6. "The Strategy forced decisionmakers to take a long-term policy perspective, which is rarely done in this environment, and to take action on these recommendations."

7. Whereas most projects were donor-driven in the past, the Strategy makes it "possible to guide donors to projects that fit within government-established programmatic priorities."

8. The "Strategy directed a lot of attention to identifying constraints on agricultural production."

9. The "Strategy strengthened the idea that the private sector should play a larger role in the agricultural sector of the economy."

CONCLUSIONS

Strategies are closely linked to prior mapping exercises and definitions of major issues. To develop innovative ways to deal with situations, participants in a strategic policy inquiry process may need to spend time conceptualizing alternatives. Techniques drawn from contingency and economic theories have proved useful in the development context and illustrate several conceptual tools for comparing alternative strategies. Special attention needs to be given to two aspects of a strategic response—sources of leadership and initiative, and procedures for monitoring activities and integrating information into the ongoing implementation process.

NOTES

1. J. Nelson, 1984, "Political Economy."
2. Kubr, 1982, *Managing*, 66.
3. Bryson, 1988, *Strategic Planning*, 168. Two useful resources in designing strategies are Lindenberg and Crosby, 1981, *Managing Development* (payoff matrix, 56–64), and Brinkerhoff, 1990, *Development Program Performance* (methods of influence, Table 3.3).
4. Israel, 1987, *Institutional Development*, 19.
5. Bryson, 1988, *Strategic Planning*, 177.
6. DPMC, 1987, *Increasing Sustainability*.
7. Korten, 1984, "Strategic Organization."
8. Bryson, 1988, *Strategic Planning*, 169–173.
9. For particularly insightful uses of contingency theory in the development context see Rondinelli, et al., 1990, *Planning Education Reforms*, and Paul, 1982, *Managing Development Programs*.
10. Macadam, et al., 1989, *Strategic Planning*, Appendix D.
11. Rondinelli, et al., 1989, "Contingency Planning," 50.
12. Stout, 1980, *Management or Control*, 101.
13. Israel, 1987, *Institutional Development*, 69–71.
14. White, 1989, "Public Management."
15. Rondinelli, et al., 1989, "Contingency Planning," 65.
16. White, 1989, "Public Management."
17. Huntington, 1987, *Institutional Development*.
18. Gruber and Mohr, 1982, "Strategic Management."
19. Paul, 1982, *Managing*, 234; Warwick, 1982, *Bitter Pills*, 41–42; Leonard, 1987, "Political Realities"; Saasa, 1985, "Public Policy-Making."
20. Austin and Ickis, 1986, "Management."
21. Staats, 1988, "Public Service," 603.
22. I am grateful to Elisabeth Shields for making this point.
23. Elmore, 1986, "Graduate Education."
24. Patton, 1986, *Utilization-Focused Evaluation;* Wholey, 1983, *Evaluation;* Weiss, 1977, "Research."
25. Paul, 1983, *Strategic Management*, 58–59.
26. Korten, 1980, "Community Organization."
27. Korten, 1987, "Third Generation NGOs."
28. Wholey, 1982, *Evaluation*.
29. The case is based on an evaluation of a planning activity in the early 1980s as reported in Jiron and Tilney, 1986, "Formulating Agricultural Policy." Quotes in the text are taken from this document.

PART THREE
POSTSCRIPT

10

Concluding Questions

Strategic policy inquiry assumes that collaboration and analysis among a number of parties and interests can integrate political and economic agendas and that the resulting sets of proposals will be more successful than those based on either logic by itself. Limited rationality, the lack of an objective economic solution, the complexity of developmental change, as well as the need to incorporate "time and place information," all place limits on a technocratic approach. At the same time, the structural bias in political systems that gives undue weight to short-term special interests places limits on a political approach. Strategic policy inquiry, described in Figure 10.1, is an alternative approach to formulating and implementing policy changes. The solid arrows indicate the proposed causal relations. If relevant parties come together and exchange ideas and information, they may reinterpret and modify their perceived interests and accept economic arguments about needed policy changes, even if these impose immediate and short-term costs. Economic arguments may also be modified to address political realities. (See the top two boxes in the middle column connected by the solid arrow.) Policies that do not emerge from such an inquiry process are less apt to successfully combine economic and political logics, as indicated by the broken arrow. Further, the model specifies a number of supporting conditions (left and right panels in Figure 10.1) that are necessary, if not sufficient, to carry out strategic policy inquiry.

The bottom half of Figure 10.1 proposes that policy reforms devised through this process are more apt to be implemented and more apt to promote sustainable economic development than are reforms that are based solely on economic logic or that are crafted solely in response to political pressures. This is especially true if the policies are promoted by external parties. As Streeten observes, even if they are well informed, such impositions "can be a kiss of death and damn the reforming groups as lackeys of foreign capital and weaken their position."[1] Externally imposed reforms and conditions and the intrusive monitoring that accompanies them will generate resent-

Figure 10.1 Strategic Policy Inquiry and Economic Development

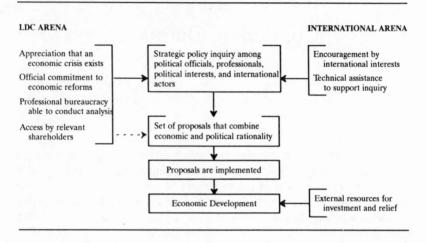

ment, will lead to uneven implementation, and will not be reinforced by necessary supporting measures or continued.

The model poses two questions: (1) Is there evidence that a strategic policy inquiry process will produce such a set of reforms, and (2) is there evidence that such reforms will be implemented and will generate sustained economic development? There is no systematic body of evidence that offers an unqualified positive answer to either. Case studies and comments by observers, however, describe successful instances of collaboration and support a positive response to the first question.

Lindenberg reviewed a number of LDC experiences and drew the following conclusions:

> Many of the more successful governments involved citizens groups in dialogue about the economic crisis and asked them to help formulate measures. In Costa Rica, President Monge mounted dialogue programs with business, labor, cooperatives, popular organizations and government officials. These groups discussed the economic crisis, the measures and possible solutions. The groups had a high sense of involvement. They were aware of and actively discussed the proposals of the IMF and the World Bank. The President also met frequently with groups from each sector, listened to their complaints and made attempts to get his economic team to take these objections into account where possible. In Jamaica, the Seaga government did not have a general reputation for consulting with key sec-

tors, but it did in one case create a multisectoral consultative commission to review a government proposal for income tax reform. The outcome was viewed as largely successful.

Later he notes that secrecy and perceptions of "rigged consultations" can be dangerous. For example, "successive Panamanian governments handled their talks with the IMF and the World Bank as highly secret negotiations. As a result, both the private sector chambers and the labor movement viewed the agreements as 'mysterious outside impositions.'"[2]

After conducting a series of workshops in 1988 on implementing policy reforms, the Economic Development Institute of the World Bank issued a report that concluded that collaborative processes needed to be expanded to involve more groups in the society.

> Getting advice from and involvement by public interest groups, associations, and the mass media is also essential. Only this permits the introduction of the measures and sacrifices required to redress economic problems and stimulate development. In short, participatory action is imperative at all levels. . . . Unfortunately, no ideal model of participation and coordination exists. Each country has to establish its own best forms of coordination and participation consistent with its traditions, political systems, and internal practices. Thus, coordination goes way beyond the traditional dialogue between the finance and planning ministries, the central bank, and the key sectoral ministries. Effective policy coordination should, as far as possible, reach some form of consensus among all sectors of the economy, public as well as private.[3]

Kaufman came to a similar conclusion after reviewing experiences in Brazil, Argentina, and Mexico. In all three systems, planning was done by a small group of top officials, leaving the plans subject to miscalculation.

> Unable to gauge the strength and reactions of key political forces, Mexican policy-makers appear to have been taken very much by surprise by the results of the 1988 presidential elections. Brazilian and Argentine authorities encountered even greater difficulties. Without institutionalized channels of consultation, neither government was able to organize a durable coalition of support around its policies. In the effort to appeal directly to mass opinion, both governments (but especially Brazil) tended to oversell their original program, then experienced erosions of credibility which impeded their effort to change course.[4]

Events in Venezuela suggest that political leaders do alter their views and redefine their policies on the basis of crisis experiences, and that the public may be willing to suspend opposition to austerity measures. During the 1970s, President Perez was an ardent populist who subsidized social services and pursued large public works projects. Severe economic problems led him to drastically alter course after his reelection in 1988. Early the next year he introduced a number of austerity measures that were followed by riots in which over 300 were killed. He has continued to let prices rise to more realistic levels, which led to an inflation rate of about 80 percent. There is vocal political opposition, but there also appears to be a growing consensus among the public that he is doing the right thing. The *Washington Post* (May 8, 1990) cites local supporters, however, who feel that he is going to have to spend more time explaining the necessity for the changes to the Venezuelan people.

Evidence related to the second question, namely the effect of strategic policy inquiry on development, is difficult to obtain because impacts on development can be assessed only in the long run. In his study of agricultural reforms in Zimbabwe, Bratton notes that many of the government's recent actions, especially supporting investments in the agricultural sector, are proving to be inefficient in the short run, but in the long run they will probably spur more widespread and sustainable economic development.[5] In the meantime, observers are tempted to measure development by actions taken rather than by results accomplished, but these can be misleading. For example, it is common to use the amount of assets transferred to private hands as an indicator of economic development. Studies indicate, however, that privatization is not always the most efficient course and that in any case is not as important as higher prices in generating increased production.[6] We need to continue to collect evidence that emphasizes results and includes measures of long-range economic development such as amount of investment, improvements in human resources, and effective institutions for generating capital and mobilizing participation in the economy.

It would be a mistake, however, to claim too much for a collaborative strategy and assume it is sufficient to generate an effective set of reforms. Evidence indicates that the conditions stipulated in Figure 10.1—especially a sense of crisis and additional resources—are critical. The Venezuela case is instructive in this regard. A severe economic crisis was clearly the catalyst for undertaking reforms. In addition, the international community responded by negotiating a 25 percent reduction in the country's $29 billion debt. The lesson is that experiences with economic disaster and additional external resources are essential ingredients in any successful reform strategy. Although there is no shortage of economic crises in LDCs, the adequacy of external resources remains problematic. In the meantime, the views of officials and proposed policies can and do change. There is evidence that collaborative policy inquiry that takes the local situation seriously and that thinks of economic change in strategic terms can improve the chances that a country will find ways to cope with its economic crises and make better use of external resources.

NOTES

1. Streeten, 1987, "Structural Adjustment," 1481.
2. Lindenberg, 1989, "Economic Adjustment," 381.
3. de Lusignan, "Development Management Discussed," *EDI Review,* July 1989, p. 3.
4. Kaufman, 1989, "Politics," 411.
5. Bratton, 1989a, "Comrades."
6. Bienen and Waterbury, 1989. "Political Economy."

References

Angle, Harold L., 1989. Research on the Management of Innovation. In A. H. Van de Ven, et al., *Psychology and Organizational Innovation*. New York: Harper and Row, Ballinger.

Ansoff, H. I., R. P. Declerck, and R. L. Hayes, eds., 1976. *From Strategic Planning to Strategic Management*. New York: John Wiley.

Argyris, Chris, 1973. Some Limits of Rational Man Organization Theory, *Public Administration Review* 33, 3, 253–267.

———, 1977. Double Loop Learning in Organizations, *Harvard Business Review* 55, 115–125.

Ascher, William, 1987. Editorial, *Policy Sciences* 21, 3–9.

Associates in Rural Development, 1989. *Bangladesh Rural and Feeder Roads: Sector Assessment*. Burlington, Vt.: Associates in Rural Development.

———, 1990. *Newsletter* 1, 1 (March).

Austin, James, and John Ickis, 1986. Management, Managers and Revolution, *World Development* 14, 7, 775–790.

Azarya, V., and N. Chazan, 1987. Disengagement from the State in Africa: Reflections on the Experience of Ghana and Guinea, *Comparative Studies in Society and History* 29, 1, 106–131.

Baier, Vicki, James March, and Harald Saetren, 1988. Implementation and Ambiguity. In James March, ed., *Decisions and Organizations*. New York: Basil Blackwell.

Bardach, Eugene, 1977. *The Implementation Game*. Cambridge, Mass.:MIT.

Bates, Robert, 1981. *Markets and States in Tropical Africa*. Berkeley: University of California Press.

Behn, Robert D., 1980. Leadership for Cutback Management: The Use of Corporate Strategy, *Public Administration Review* 40, 6, 613–620.

———, 1988. Management by Groping Along, *Journal of Policy Analysis and Management* 8 (Fall).

Bello, W., and C. Saunt, 1987. International Debt Crisis, Year Five, *Christianity and Crisis* (November 23), 403–413.

Bem, Daryl, 1970. *Beliefs, Attitudes, and Human Affairs*. Belmont, Calif.: Wadsworth.

Bienen, Henry, and Mark Gersovitz, 1985. Economic Stabilization, Conditionality, and Political Stability, *International Organization* 39, 4, 729–754.

Bienen, Henry, and John Waterbury, 1989. The Political Economy of Privatization in Developing Countries, *World Development* 17, 5, 617–632.

Blunt, Peter, 1983. *Organizational Theory and Behaviour: An African Perspective.* New York: Longman.

Bossert, T., et al., 1987. *Sustainability of U.S. Supported Health Programs in Honduras.* Washington D.C.: Agency for International Development, Center for Development Information and Development.

Boyer, William, and Byong Man Ahn, 1989. "Local Government and Development Administration: The Case of Rural South Korea," *Planning and Administration* 16: 2, 21–29.

Bozeman, Barry, and David Landsbergen, 1989. Truth and Credibility in Sincere Policy Analysis, *Evaluation Review* 13, 4, 355–79.

Bradford, Colin, Jr., 1986. East Asian 'Models': Myths and Lessons. In John Lewis and Valeriana Kallab, eds., *Development Strategies Reconsidered.* New Brunswick, N.J.: Transaction Books, in cooperation with Overseas Development Council.

Bratton, Michael, 1986. Farmer Organizations and Food Production in Zimbabwe, *World Development* 14, 3, 367–384.

———, 1989a. The Comrades and the Countryside: The Politics of Agricultural Policy in Zimbabwe, *World Politics* 12, 2, 174–202.

———, 1989b. The Politics of Government-NGO Relations in Africa, *World Development* 17, 4, 569–587.

Brewer, Garry, and Peter deLeon, 1983. *The Foundations of Policy Analysis.* Homewood, Ill.: Dorsey.

Brinkerhoff, Derick, 1988. Implementing Integrated Rural Development in Haiti, *Canadian Journal of Development Studies* 9, 1, 63–79.

———, 1990. *Improving Development Program Performance: Guidelines for Managers.* Boulder, Colo.: Lynne Rienner Publishers.

Brinkerhoff, Derick, and Arthur Goldsmith, 1988. The Challenge of Administrative Reform in Haiti, *International Review of Administrative Sciences* 54, 1, 89–114.

Brinkerhoff, Derick, and Richard L. Hopkins, 1989. Institutional Dimensions of Education Sector Lending: Guidelines for Management and Sustainability Assessment, p. 23. Washington, D.C.: World Bank, Population and Human Resources Department.

Brinkerhoff, Derick, and Marcus Ingle, 1989. Integrating Blueprint and Process: A Structured Flexibility Approach to Development Management, *Public Administration and Development* 9, 487–503.

Brinkerhoff, Derick, and E. Philip Morgan, 1989. The Dance of Structural Adjustment: Policy Reform as Partisan Mutual Adjustment. Paper delivered at the 50th National Conference of the American Society for Public Administration, Miami, Florida (April 9–13).

Brown, L. David, and Jane Covey, 1987. Development Organizations and Organization Development. In W.E. Pasmore and R. Woodman, eds., *Research in Organization Development,* Vol. 1. Greenwich, Conn.: JAI Press.

Bruton, Henry, 1985. The Search for a Development Economics, *World Development* 13, 10/11, 1099–1124.

Bryant, Coralie, and Louise G. White, 1982. *Managing Development in the Third World.* Boulder, Colo.: Westview Press.

Bryson, John, 1988. *Strategic Planning for Public and Nonprofit Organizations.* San Francisco: Jossey-Bass.

Bryson, John, and Kimberly Boal, 1983. Strategic Management in a Metropolitan Area, *Academy of Management Proceedings* (August), 332–336.

Bryson, John, and William Roering, 1988. Initiation of Strategic Planning by Governments, *Public Administration Review* 48, 6, 995–1004.

Buchanan, James, and Gordon Tullock, 1962. *The Calculus of Consent.* Ann Arbor: University of Michigan.

Calavan, Michael, 1984. Appropriate Administration: Creating a 'Space' Where Local Initiative and Voluntarism Can Grow. In R. Gorman, ed., *Private Voluntary Organizations As Agents of Development,* 215–250. Boulder, Colo.: Westview Press.

Callaghy, Thomas, 1989. Toward State Capability and Embedded Liberalism in the Third World: Lessons for Adjustment. In Joan Nelson, ed., *Fragile Coalitions.* New Brunswick, N.J.: Transaction Books.

———, 1990. Lost Between State and Market. In Joan Nelson, ed., *Economic Crisis and Policy Choice: The Politics of Adjustment in the Third World.* Princeton: Princeton University Press.

Chambers, Robert, 1980. *Rural Poverty Unperceived,* World Bank Staff Working Paper No. 400. Washington, D.C.: World Bank.

Christakis, Alexander, 1985. A Role for Systems Scientists in the Age of Design. Fairfax, Va.: Center for Interactive Managment, George Mason University. Mimeo.

Chu, Yun-han, 1989. State Structure and Economic Adjustment of the East Asian Newly Industrializing Countries, *International Organization* 43, 4 (Autumn).

Church, Phillip, and Roberto Castro, 1988. *Formulating Agricultural Policy in a Complex Institutional Environment.* Washington, D.C.: Abt Associates.

Churchman, C. West, 1968. *The Systems Approach.* New York: Dell.

Cohen, John, Merilee Grindle, and John Thomas, 1985. Foreign Aid and Conditions Precedent: Political and Bureaucratic Dimensions, *World Development* 13, 12, 1211–1230.

Cornia, Giovanni, Richard Jolly, and Frances Stewart, 1987. *Adjustment with a Human Face.* New York: Oxford.

Dahlman, Carl, Bruce Ross-Larson, and Larry Westphal, 1987. Managing Technological Development: Lessons from the Newly Industrializing Countries, *World Development* 15, 6, 759–775.

deBono, Edward, 1970. *Lateral Thinking.* New York: Harper.

Delbecq, Andre, Andrew Van de Ven, and David Gustafson, 1975. *Group Techniques for Program Planning.* Glenview, Ill.: Scott, Foresman.

Delp, Peter, Arne Thesen, Juzar Motiwalla, and Neelakantan Seshadri, 1977. *Systems Tools for Project Planning.* Bloomington, Ind.: International Development Institute.

Deyo, Frederick, 1987. Coalitions, Institutions, and Linkage Sequencing—Toward a Strategic Capacity Model of East Asian Development. In Frederic Deyo, ed., *The Political Economy of New Asian Industrialism.* Ithaca, N.Y.: Cornell University Press.

Diallo, Aliou, Mamadou Kante, and E. Philip Morgan, 1988. Organization Development and Management Improvement: Ministry of Agriculture and Animal Resources, Republic of Guinea. Washington, D.C.: National Association of Schools of Public Affairs and Administration.

Dichter, Thomas, 1987. *Development Management: Plain or Fancy? Sorting Out Some Muddles.* Norwalk, Conn.: Technoserve.

DPMC (Development Project Management Center), 1987. With International Development Management Center. *Increasing the Sustainability of Development Assistance Efforts.* Washington, D.C.: Agency for International Development.

Eadie, Douglas, 1983. Putting a Powerful Tool to Practical Use: The Application of Strategic Planning in the Public Sector, *Public Administration Review* 43, 447–452.

Eadie, Douglas, and Roberta Steinbacher, 1985. Strategic Agenda Management: A Marriage of Organizational Development and Strategic Planning, *Public Administration Review* 45, 3, 424–430.

ECA (Economic Commission for Africa), 1989. *African Alternative to Structural Adjustment Programmes: A Framework for Transformation and Recovery.* New York: United Nations.

Eckaus, R. S., 1986. How the IMF Lives with Its Conditionality, *Policy Sciences* 19, 237–252.

Edwards, Daniel, 1988. *Managing Institutional Development Projects: Water and Sanitation Sector.* WASH Technical Report No. 49. Washington, D.C.: Agency for International Development.

Eele, Graham, 1989. The Organization and Management of Statistical Services in Africa, *World Development* 17, 3, 431–438.

Elmore, Richard, 1986. Graduate Education in Public Management: Working the Seams of Government, *Journal of Policy Analysis and Management* 6 (January), 66–83.

Esman, Milton, 1978. *Landlessness and Near Landlessness.* Ithaca, N.Y.: Cornell University Press.

———, 1989. The Maturing of Development Administration, *Public Administration and Development* 8, 125–134.

Esman, Milton, and Norman Uphoff, 1984. *Local Organizations, Intermediaries in Rural Development.* Ithaca, N.Y.: Cornell University Press.

Fiol, F. M., and M. A. Lyles, 1985. Organizational Learning, *Academy of Management Review* 10, 4, 803–813.

Gellar, Sheldon, 1985. Pitfalls of Top-Down Development Planning and Macro-Economic Analyses. Paper presented at the Conference on Institutional Analysis and Development, Washington, D.C.: Agency for International Development (May 21–22).

Gilpin, Robert, 1987. *The Political Economy of International Relations.* Princeton: Princeton University Press.

Golden, Olivia, 1989. Innovation in Public Sector Human Services Programs: The Implications of Innovation by 'Groping Along.' Cambridge, Mass.: J. F. K. School of Government.

Goldsmith, Arthur, 1988. The Management of Institutional Innovation: Lessons from Transferring the Land Grant Model to India, *Public Administration and Development* 8, 317–330.

Gonzalez-Vega, C., 1979. *Invierno: Innovation in Credit and in Rural Development.* Washington, D.C.: Agency for International Development.

Good, Kenneth, 1986. Systemic Agricultural Mismanagement: The 1985 'Bumper' Harvest in Zambia, *The Journal of Modern African Studies* 24, 1, 257–284.

Green, Reginald, and C. Allison, 1986. The World Bank's Agenda for Accelerated Development: Dialectics, Doubts and Dialogues. In John Ravenhill, ed., *Africa in Economic Crisis*, 60–84. New York: Columbia University Press.

Grindle, Merilee, ed., 1980. *Politics and Policy Implementation in the Third World.* Princeton: Princeton University Press.

Grindle, Merilee, and John Thomas, 1989. Policy Makers, Policy Choices, and Policy Outcomes: The Political Economy of Reform in Developing Countries, *Policy Sciences* 22, 213–248.

Gruber, Robert, and Mary Mohr, 1982. Strategic Management for Multipurpose Nonprofit Organizations, *California Management Review* 24, 3 (Spring), 15–22.

Hage, Jerald, and Kurt Finsterbusch, 1987. *Organizational Change as a Development Strategy.* Boulder, Colo.: Lynne Rienner Publishers.

Haggard, Stephan, 1985. The Politics of Adjustment: Lessons from the IMF's Extended Fund Facility, *International Organization* 39, 3, 505–534.

Haggard, Stephan, and Robert Kaufman, 1989. The Politics of Stabilization and Structural Adjustment. In Jeffrey D. Sachs, ed., *Developing Country Debt and Economic Performance*. Chicago: University of Chicago Press.

Hammermesh, Richard, ed., 1983. *Strategic Management*. New York: John Wiley.

Hart, Stuart, Mark Boroush, Gorden Enk, and William Hornick, 1985. Managing Complexity Through Consensus Mapping, *Academy of Management Review* 10, 3, 587–600.

Hayek, Frederick A., 1945. The Use of Knowledge in Society, *The American Economic Review* 35, 4 (September), 519–530.

Haykin, Stephen, 1987. *Policy Reform Programs in Africa: A Preliminary Assessment of Impacts*. Washington, D.C.: USAID, Bureau for Africa.

Haynes, Jeff, Trevor Parfitt, and Stephen Riley, 1987. "Debt in Sub-Saharan Africa: The Local Politics of Stabilization," *African Affairs* 86, 344, 343–366.

Healy, Paul, 1986. Interpretive Policy Inquiry, *Policy Sciences* 19, 382–396.

Heaver, Richard, 1982. *Bureaucratic Politics and Incentives in the Management of Rural Development*. World Bank Staff Working Paper No. 537. Washington, D.C.: World Bank.

Heaver, Richard, and Arturo Israel, 1986. *Country Commitment to Development Projects*. World Bank Discussion Paper No. 4. Washington, D.C.: World Bank.

Heclo, Hugh, 1974. *Modern Social Policy in Britain and Sweden*. New Haven: Yale University Press.

Helleiner, Gerald K., 1986a. IMF and Africa in the 1980s, *Canadian Journal of African Studies* 17, 1.

————, 1986b. Policy-Based Program Lending: A Look at the Bank's New Role. In Richard E. Feinberg and contributors, *Between Two Worlds: The World Bank's Next Decade*. New Brunswick, N.J.: Transaction Books, in cooperation with the Overseas Development Council.

Hirschman, Albert E., 1981. *Exit, Voice and Loyalty*. Washington, D.C.: Brookings.

————, 1984. *Getting Ahead Collectively*. New York: Pergamon.

————, 1988. The Principle of Conservation and Mutation of Social Energy. In Sheldon Annis and Peter Hakim, *Direct to the Poor*. Boulder, Colo.: Lynne Rienner Publishers.

Honadle, George, 1982. Rapid Reconnaissance for Development Administration: Mapping and Moulding Organizational Landscapes, *World Development* 10, 8, 633–649.

Honadle, George, and Jerry VanSant, 1985. *Implementation for Sustainability*. Hartford: Conn.: Kumarian.

Horowitz, Donald, 1989. Is There a Third-World Policy Process? *Policy Sciences* 22, 197–212.

Horowitz, Irving Louis, 1987. The "Roshomon Effect": Ideological Proclivities and Political Dilemmas of the IMF. In Robert Myers, ed., *The Political Morality of the International Monetary Fund*. New Brunswick, N.J.: Transaction Books.

Horton, D., 1986. Assessing the Impact of International Agricultural Research and Development Programs, *World Development* 14, 4, 453–468.

Huntington, Richard, 1987. *Accelerating Institutional Development*. Washington, D.C.: International Science and Technology Institute.

Hyden, Goren, 1983. *No Shortcuts to Progress*. Berkeley: University of California Press.

Ilchman, Warren, and Norman Uphoff, 1969. *The Political Economy of Change*. Berkeley: University of California.

Ingle, Marcus, 1979. *Implementing Development Programs: A State of the Art Review.* Syracuse: Syracuse University.

———, 1985. Integrating Management and Production: Improving Performance in Portugal's Ministry of Agriculture. Paper presented at the forty-sixth national conference, American Society of Public Administration, Indianapolis (March).

Israel, Arturo, 1987. *Institutional Development.* Baltimore: Johns Hopkins University Press.

Janis, Irving, 1972. *Victims of Groupthink.* Boston: Houghton, Mifflin.

———, 1989. *Crucial Decisions.* New York: Free Press.

Jiron, Rolando, and John Tilney, Jr., 1986. *Formulating Agricultural Policy in a Complex Institutional Environment: The Case of Sri Lanka.* Washington, D.C.: Abt Associates.

Johnson, Chalmers, 1987. Political Institutions and Economic Performance: The Government-Business Relationship in Japan, South Korea, and Taiwan. In Frederic Deyo, ed., *The Political Economy of New Asian Industrialism.* Ithaca, N.Y.: Cornell University Press.

Jones, Andrea, and Wayne Clyma, 1986. An Approach to Management Improvement for Irrigated Agriculture: The Management Training and Planning Program for Command Water Management, Pakistan, *Water Management Review* (Spring).

———, 1988. *Improving the Management of Irrigated Agriculture: The Management Training and Planning Program for Command Water Management, Pakistan,* WMS Professional Paper No. 3. Fort Collins, Colo.: Colorado State University.

Kahler, Miles, 1989. International Financial Institutions and the Politics of Adjustment. In Joan Nelson, *Fragile Coalitions: The Politics of Economic Adjustment.* New Brunswick, N.J.: Transaction Books, in cooperation with Overseas Development Council.

———, 1990. Orthodoxy and Its Alternatives: Explaining Approaches to Stabilization and Adjustment. In Joan Nelson, ed., *Economic Crisis and Policy Choice: The Politics of Economic Adjustment in the Third World.* Princeton: Princeton University Press.

———, ed., 1986. *The Politics of International Debt.* Ithaca, N.Y.: Cornell University Press.

Katzenstein, Peter, 1985. Small Nations in an Open International Economy. In Peter Evans, Dietrich Rueschemeyer, and Theda Skocpol, eds., *Bringing the State Back In.* New York: Cambridge University Press.

Kaufman, Robert, 1989. The Politics of Economic Adjustment Policy in Argentina, Brazil, and Mexico: Experiences in the 1980s and Challenges for the Future, *Policy Sciences* 22, 395–413.

Kettering, Merlyn, 1985. *Action-Training for Development Management.* Washington, D.C.: United States Department of Agriculture, Development Program Management Center (June).

———, 1987. *Microcomputer Based Information Systems for Public Financial Management in Kenya.* Alexandria, Va.: Thunder and Associates.

Kiggundu, Moses N., 1989. *Managing Organizations in Developing Countries.* Hartford, Conn.: Kumarian.

Killick, Tony, 1986. Twenty-five Years in Development: The Rise and Impending Decline of Market Solutions, *Development Policy Review* 4, 99–116.

Kingdon, John W., 1984. *Agendas, Alternatives, and Public Policies.* Boston: Little, Brown.

Kiser, Larry, and Elinor Ostrom, 1982. The Three Worlds of Action. In Elinor Ostrom, ed., *Strategies of Political Inquiry.* Beverly Hills: Sage.

Klitgaard, Robert, 1989. Incentive Myopia, *World Development* 17, 4, 447–459.

Kohli, Atul, 1989. Politics of Economic Liberalization in India, *World Development* 17, 3, 305–328.

Korten, David, 1980. Community Organization and Rural Development: A Learning Process Approach, *Public Administration Review* 40, 480–511.

——, 1982. *The Working Group as a Mechanism for Managing Bureaucratic Reorientation*. Working Paper No. 4. Washington, D.C.: National Association of Schools of Public Affairs and Administration.

——, 1984. Strategic Organization for People-Centered Development, *Public Administration Review* 44, 4, 341–352.

——, 1987. Third Generation NGO Strategies: A Key to People-Centered Development, *World Development* 15, Supplement (Fall), 145–160.

——, 1990. *Getting to the 21st Century: Voluntary Action and the Global Agenda*. Hartford, Conn.: Kumarian.

Korten, David, and George Carner, 1984. Planning Frameworks for People-Centered Development. In David Korten and Rudi Klauss, eds., *People-Centered Development*. Hartford, Conn.: Kumarian.

Krueger, Anne, 1979. The Political Economy of the Rent Seeking Society, *The American Economic Review* 64 (June), 291–303.

Kubr, Milan, 1982. *Managing a Management Development Institution*. Geneva: International Labor Organization.

Kydd, Jonathan, 1986. Changes in Zambian Agricultural Policy Since 1983: Problems of Liberalization and Agrarianization, *Development Policy Review* 4, 233–259.

Lamb, Geoffrey, 1986. *Institutional Dimensions of Economic Policy Management*. Washington, D.C.: World Bank.

Lancaster, Carol, 1988. Political Economy and Policy Reform in Sub-Saharan Africa. In Stephen Commins, ed., *Africa's Development Challenges and the World Bank*. Boulder, Colo.: Lynne Rienner Publishers.

Landau, Martin, 1986. On Decision Strategies and Management Structures, Committee on the Study of Public Organizations, University of California, Berkeley.

Lee, Man-Gap, ed., 1981. *Toward a New Community Life: Reports of International Research Seminar on the Saemaul Movement*. Seoul: Seoul National University.

Lele, Uma, Nicolas Van De Walle, and Mathurin Gbetibouo, 1989. *Cotton in Africa: An Analysis of Differences in Performance*. Managing Agricultural Development in Africa. Discussion Paper No. 7. Washington, D.C.: World Bank.

Leonard, David, 1987. The Political Realities of African Management, *World Development* 15, 899–910.

——, 1989. *The Secrets of Successful African Governance*. Berkeley: University of California Press.

Levine, Charles, 1985. Police Management in the 1980s: From Decrementalism to Strategic Thinking, *Public Administration Review* 45, 6, 691–699.

Lewis, John P., et al., 1988. *Strengthening the Poor: What Have We Learned?* New Brunswick, N.J.: Transaction Books, in cooperation with Overseas Development Council.

Lindblom, Charles, 1959. The Science of Muddling Through, *Public Administration Review* 19 (Spring), 79–88.

Lindenberg, Marc, 1988. Central America: Crisis and Economic Strategy 1930–1985, Lessons From History, *The Journal of Developing Areas* 22 (January), 155–178.

——, 1989. Making Economic Adjustment Work, *Policy Sciences* 22, 359–394.

Lindenberg, Marc, and Benjamin Crosby, 1981. *Managing Development: The Political Dimension*. Hartford, Conn.: Kumarian.

Lovrich, Nicholas, 1989. The Simon/Argyris Debate: Bounded Rationality Versus

Self-Actualization Concepts of Human Nature, *Public Administration Quarterly* (Winter), 452–483.

Macadam, Robert, Gregg Baker, and Kenneth Shapiro, 1989. *Strategic Planning for Sustainability*. Falls Church, Va.: Pragma Corp.

Macintosh, Maureen, 1986. Economic Policy Context and Adjustment Options in Mozambique, *Development and Change* 17, 557–581.

Mahler, Julianne, 1987. Structured Decision Making in Public Organizations, *Public Administration Review* 47, 4, 336–342.

March, James, and Johan Olsen, 1984. The New Institutionalism: Organizational Factors in American Life, *American Political Science Review* 78, 3, 734–749.

———, 1989. *Rediscovering Institutions*. New York: Free Press.

Maxwell, S., 1986. Farming Systems Research: Hitting a Moving Target, *World Development* 14, 1, 65–77.

McCleary, William A. 1989. Policy Implementation Under Adjustment Lending, *Finance and Development* 26, 1, 32–34.

Meesook, O., and P. Suebsaeng, 1985. Wage Policy and the Structure of Wages and Employment in Zambia. Washington, D.C.: World Bank. Mimeo.

Mickelwait, Donald, 1980. *Technical Assistance for Integrated Rural Development: A Management Team Approach*. IRD Working Paper No. 3. Washington, D.C.: Development Alternatives, Inc.

Miles, Matthew, and A. Michael Huberman, 1984. *Qualitative Data Analysis*. Beverly Hills: Sage.

Miner, Frederick, 1979. A Comparative Analysis of Three Diverse Group Decision Making Approaches, *Academy of Management Journal* 22, 1, 81–93.

———, 1984. Group Versus Individual Decision Making, *Organizational Behavior and Human Performance* 33, 112–124.

Mitra, Radja, 1989. The Social Market Economy Paradigm: Lessons from the Early Nordic Development Experience. Washington, D.C.: World Bank, Special Economic Office. Mimeo.

Mitroff, Ian, and James Emshoff, 1979. On Strategic Assumption Making, *Academy of Management Review* 4, 1, 1–12.

Mittleman, James, 1988. *Out from Underdevelopment*. New York: St. Martin's Press.

Montgomery, John, 1986a. Bureaucratic Politics in Southern Africa, *Public Administration Review* 46, 5, 407–413.

———, 1986b. Life at the Apex: The Functions of Permanent Secretaries in Nine Southern African Countries, *Public Administration and Development* 6, 3, 211–222.

Moris, Jon R., 1981. *Managing Induced Rural Development*. Bloomington, Ind.: International Development Institute.

Mosley, Paul, 1986. Agricultural Performance in Kenya Since 1970: Has the World Bank Got It Right? *Development and Change* 17, 513–530.

National Research Council, 1986. *Common Property Resources Management*. Washington, D.C.: National Academy Press.

Nellis, John, 1986. *Public Enterprises in Sub-Saharan Africa*. Washington, D.C.: World Bank.

Nelson, Joan, 1984. The Political Economy of Stabilization: Commitment, Capacity, and Public Response, *World Development* 12, 10, 983–1006.

———, 1986. The Diplomacy of Policy Based Lending, in Richard Feinberg, ed., *Between Two Worlds: The World Bank's Next Decade*, 67–86. New Brunswick, N.J.: Transaction Books, in cooperation with Overseas Development Council.

———, 1989. The Politics of Long-Haul Economic Reform. In *Fragile Coalitions: The Politics of Economic Adjustment*. New Brunswick, N.J.: Transaction Books, in cooperation with Overseas Development Council.

Nelson, Richard, 1977. *The Moon and the Ghetto.* New York: W. W. Norton.

———, 1989. On Technological Capabilities and Their Acquisition. Paper delivered at the Conference on Science and Technology Policy, sponsored by the Economic Growth Center, Yale University, March. Mimeo.

Nelson, Richard, and Sydney Winter, 1982. *An Evolutionary Theory of Economic Change.* Cambridge, Mass.: Harvard University Press.

Nicholas, Peter, 1988. *The World Bank's Lending for Adjustment.* Washington, D.C.: World Bank.

Nicholson, Norman, 1989. The State of the Art. In Vincent Ostrom, D. Feeny, and H. Picht, eds., *Rethinking Institutional Analysis and Development,* 3–39. San Francisco: International Center for Economic Growth.

Nicholson, Norman, and Edwin Connerley, 1989. The Impending Crisis in Development Administration, *International Journal of Public Administration* 12, 385–425.

North, Douglass, 1981. *Structure and Change in Economic History.* New York: W. W. Norton.

OED, 1988. *Operations Evaluation Department Annual Review 1988.* Washington, D.C.: World Bank.

Office of Technology Assessment (OTA), 1988. *Enhancing Agriculture in Africa* (OYA-F-356). Washington, D.C.: Government Printing Office.

Ostrom, Elinor, Larry Schroeder, and Susan Wynne, 1990. *Institutional Incentives and Rural Infrastructure Sustainability.* Burlington, Vt.: Associates in Rural Development.

Ostrom, Vincent, David Feeny, and Hartmut Picht, eds., 1988. *Rethinking Institutional Analysis and Development.* San Francisco: International Center for Economic Growth.

O'Toole, Laurence J., Jr., 1986. Policy Recommendations for Multi-Actor Implementation: An Assessment of the Field, *Journal of Public Policy* (April-June), 181–210.

Patton, Michael, 1981. *Creative Evaluation.* Beverly Hills: Sage.

———, 1986. *Utilization-Focused Evaluation,* 2d ed. Beverly Hills: Sage, 1986.

Paul, Samuel, 1982. *Managing Development Programs: The Lessons of Success.* Boulder, Colo.: Westview Press.

———, 1983. *Strategic Management of Development Programmes.* Geneva: International Labor Organization.

———, 1989. Institutional Reforms in Sector Adjustment Operations. Washington, D.C.: World Bank (March). Mimeo.

Polanyi, Karl, 1944. *The Great Transformation.* Boston: Beacon.

Ravenhill, John, 1986. Africa's Continuing Crises: The Elusiveness of Development. In John Ravenhill, ed., *Africa in Economic Crisis,* 1–43. New York: Columbia University Press.

Reich, Robert, 1983. *The Next American Frontier.* New York: Penguin.

Rondinelli, Dennis, 1987. *Development Administration and U.S. Foreign Aid Policy.* Boulder, Colo.: Lynne Rienner Publishers.

Rondinelli, Dennis, James McCullough, and Ronald Johnson, 1989. Analysing Decentralization Policies in Developing Countries: A Political-Economy Framework, *Development and Change* 20, 57–87.

Rondinelli, Dennis, John Middleton, and Adriaan Verspoor, 1989. Contingency Planning for Innovative Projects, *Journal of the American Planning Association* 55, 1, 454–457.

———, 1990. *Planning Education Reforms in Developing Countries.* Durham, N.C.: Duke University.

Ruttan, Vernon, 1982. *Agricultural Research Policy*. Minneapolis: University of Minnesota Press.

———, 1986. Assistance to Expand Agricultural Production, *World Development* 14, 1, 39–63.

Ruttan, Vernon, and Y. Hayami, 1983. Toward a Theory of Induced Institutional Innovation, *Journal of Development Studies* 20, 4, 203–223.

Saasa, Oliver, 1985. Public Policy-Making in Developing Countries: The Utility of Contemporary Decision-Making Models, *Public Administration and Development* 5, 4, 309–321.

Sabatier, Paul, 1986. Top-Down and Bottom-Up Approaches to Implementation Research, *Journal of Public Policy* (January-March), 21–48.

———, 1988. An Advocacy Coalition Framework of Policy Change and The Role of Policy-Oriented Learning Therein, *Policy Sciences* 21, 129–168.

Sachs, Jeffrey, 1989. *New Approaches to the Latin American Debt Crisis*. Essays in International Finance No. 174. Princeton, N.J.: Princeton University Department of Economics.

Sandbrook, Richard, 1986. The State and Economic Stagnation in Tropical Africa, *World Development* 14, 3, 319–332.

Sanwal, Mukul, 1988. Designing Training for Development Administration: Lessons from India's Experience, *Public Administration and Development* 8, 331–344.

Scrimshaw, Susan C., and Elena Hurtado, 1987. *Rapid Assessment Procedures for Nutrition and Primary Health Care*. Tokyo: United Nations University.

Shirley, M., 1988. The Experience with Privatization, *Finance and Development* 25 (September), 34–35.

Silverman, Jerry, Merlyn Kettering, and I. D. Schmidt, 1986. *Action-Planning Workshops for Development Management: Guidelines*. Technical Paper No. 56. Washington, D.C.: World Bank.

Simon, Herbert, 1985. Human Nature in Politics, *American Political Science Review* 79, 293–304.

Skocpol, Theda, 1985. Bringing the State Back In: Strategies of Analysis in Current Research. In Peter Evans, Dietrich Rueschemeyer and Theda Skocpol, eds., *Bringing the State Back In*, 3–37. Cambridge: Cambridge University Press.

Smith, William, Francis Lethem, and Ben Thoolen, 1980. *The Design of Organizations in Rural Development Projects*. World Bank Staff Working Paper No. 375. Washington, D.C.: World Bank.

Staats, Elmer, 1988. Public Service and the Public Interest, *Public Administration Review* 48, 2, 601–605.

Stone, Clarence, 1980. The Implementation of Social Programs, *Journal of Social Issues* 36, 13–34.

Stout, Russell, 1980. *Management or Control*. Bloomington: Indiana University.

Streeten, Paul, 1987. Structural Adjustment: A Survey of Issues and Options, *World Development* 15, 12, 1469–1482.

Sukin, H., 1987. Zambia: 1987's Development Tragedy. Washington, D.C.: Agency for International Development.

Sweet, Charles F., and P. F. Weisel, 1979. Process Versus Blueprint Models for Designing Rural Development Projects. In George Honadle and Rudi Klauss, eds., *International Development Administration: Implementation Analysis for Development Projects*. 127–145. New York: Praeger.

Taylor, Lance, 1987. IMF Conditionality: Incomplete Theory, Policy Malpractice. In Robert J. Myers, ed., *The Political Morality of the International Monetary Fund*, Vol. 3 of Carnegie Council on Ethics and International Affairs. New Brunswick, N.J.: Transaction Books.

Tendler, Judith, 1982. *Turning Private Voluntary Organizations into Development Agencies*. AID Program Evaluation Discussion Paper No. 12, Washington, D.C.: Agency for International Development.

Thomson, James, 1981. Public Choice Analysis of Institutional Constraints on Firewood Production in the West African Sahel. In C. S. Russell and Norman Nicholson, eds., *Public Choice and Rural Development*. Washington, D.C.: Resources for the Future.

Timberlake, L. 1985. *Africa in Crisis: The Causes, the Cures of Environmental Bankruptcy*. Washington, D.C.: International Institute for Environment and Development, Earthscan.

Torgerson, Douglas, 1986. Between Knowledge and Politics, *Policy Sciences* 19, 33–59.

Uphoff, Norman, 1982. Introduction to East Asian Cases. In Norman Uphoff, ed., *Rural Development and Local Organization in Asia: East Asia*, Vol. 2. Delhi: Macmillan India.

———, 1985. Peoples' Participation in Water Management: Gal Oya, Sri Lanka. In J. Garcia-Zamor, ed., *Public Participation in Development Planning and Management*, 131–178. Boulder: Westview Press.

———, 1986. *Local Institutional Development*. Hartford, Conn.: Kumarian.

———, 1987. Drawing on Social Energy in Project Implementation: A Learning Process Experience in Sri Lanka. Paper delivered at annual meeting of the American Society for Public Administration, Boston (March).

Uphoff, Norman, M. L. Wickramasinghe, and C. M. Wijayarartne, 1990. "'Optimum' Participation in Irrigation Management," *Human Organization* 49, 1: 26–40.

USAID (U.S. Agency for International Development), 1987. *Interim Country Development Strategy Statement, Fiscal Years 1988–1990*. Washington, D.C.: Agency for International Development (February 24).

Van Arkadie, Brian, 1986. Some Realities of Adjustment, *Development and Change* 17, 3, 371–386.

Vondal, Patricia, 1987. A Review of Social and Institutional Analyses in Non-Project Assistance, Bureau for Africa, Office of Development and Planning. Washington, D.C.: Agency for International Development.

Warwick, Donald, 1982. *Bitter Pills*. New York: Cambridge University Press.

Wechsler, Barton, and Robert Backoff, 1986. Policy Making and Administration in State Agencies: Strategic Management Approaches, *Public Administration Review* 46, 4, 321–327.

Weidemann, Wesley, et al., 1987. *Zambian Agricultural Sector Policy Impact Assessment*. Washington, D.C.: Agency for International Development.

Weintraub, Sidney, 1989. Policy-Based Assistance: A Historical Perspective. Washington, D.C.: Agency For International Development (July 20). Mimeo.

Weiss, Carol, 1977. Research for Policy's Sake: The Enlightenment Function of Social Research, *Policy Analysis* 3, 531–545.

Weiss, Janet, 1987. Pathways to Cooperation Among Public Agencies, *Journal of Policy Analysis and Management* 7, 1, 94–117.

White, Louise G., 1982. Improving the Goal-Setting Process in Local Government, *Public Administration Review* 42, 1, 77–83.

———, 1986. *Managing Development Programs*. AID Evaluation Special Study No. 38. Washington, D.C.: Agency for International Development.

———, 1987. *Creating Opportunities for Change*, Boulder, Colo.: Lynne Rienner Publishers.

———, 1989. Public Management in a Pluralistic Arena, *Public Administration Review* 49, 6, 522–532.

————, 1990a. Implementing Economic Policy Reforms, *World Development* 18, 1 (January).

————, 1990b. Policy Reforms in Sub-Saharan Africa: Conditions for Establishing a Dialogue, *Studies in Comparative International Development* 25, 2.

————, 1990c. Agricultural Research, *Journal of Developing Areas* (July).

————, 1990d, Global Policy Studies and the Nation State. In Stuart Nagel and Marvin Soroos, eds., *Global Policy Studies*. New York: Macmillan.

Whitehead, Laurence, 1989, Democratization and Disinflation: A Comparative Approach. In Joan Nelson, *Fragile Coalitions*. New Brunswick, N.J.: Transaction Books.

Wholey, Joseph, 1983. *Evaluation and Effective Public Management*. Boston: Little, Brown.

Williamson, Oliver, 1975. *Markets and Hierarchies*. New York: Free Press.

Wilson, Kathleen, and George Morren, Jr., 1990. *Systems Approaches for Improvement in Agriculture and Resource Management*. New York: Macmillian.

World Bank, 1986. *World Development Report 1986*. Washington, D.C.: World Bank.

————, 1987. Staff Appraisal Report, Republic of Guinea, National Seeds Project. Washington, D.C.: World Bank.

————, 1988. *Adjustment Lending: An Evaluation of Ten Years of Experience*. Washington, D.C.: World Bank.

————, 1989a. *Africa's Adjustment and Growth in the 1980s*. Washington, D.C.: World Bank and United Nations Development Programme.

————, 1989b. *Sub-Saharan Africa: From Crisis to Sustainable Growth*. Washington, D.C.: World Bank.

————, 1990. *Poverty, World Development Report 1990*. Washington, D.C.: World Bank.

Index

About the Book
and the Author

The century is closing with an outpouring of experiments in political and economic reform around the globe. Most reform efforts are carried out from the top. Democratic institutions and market economies, however, require change in attitudes and institutional capacity throughout a society. These kinds of changes cannot be brought about from the top; they depend on the widespread collaboration and involvement of groups and individuals.

Implementing Policy Reforms makes this case by examining the experiences of Third World countries as they attempt to make far-reaching structural changes to liberalize their economies. The changes are politically unpopular, their impacts are still uncertain, and they impose major demands on weak political organizations. In this context, it is tempting—both for leaders inside the countries and for outsiders offering assistance—to look for technocratic solutions and to impose them on the society.

This study proposes an alternative—a process for implementing reforms that engages the participants in diagnosing their situations and designing fitting policy responses and implementation strategies. Part One develops a rationale for the process, drawing from theories of policy analysis, strategic management, and bounded rationality. This theoretical grounding ensures that the process is not reduced to a set of techniques. Part Two, based on recent experiences with technical assistance to LDCs, describes in detail steps for carrying out the process.

Addressing those involved in designing policy reforms or in providing technical assistance, Louise White integrates the lessons of experience within LDCs with recent theoretical innovations to present a strategic management approach to effecting positive and lasting change.

LOUISE WHITE is associate professor in the Department of Public Affairs at George Mason University.